Best in the Northei

The pioneering 1910 Rugby
tour of Australia and Nev

Tom Mather

London League Publications Ltd

Best in the Northern Union

© Tom Mather. Foreword © Sean Fagan.

The moral right of Tom Mather be identified as the author has been asserted.

Cover design © Stephen McCarthy.

Front cover: The Northern Union tourists in formal attire
Back cover: The tourists on their arrival in New Zealand.
Title page: The 1910 Northern Union tourists. Back: T. Helm, G. Ruddick,
F. Shugars, R. Ramsdale, E. Curzon, J. Leytham, W. Winstanley; third row:
F. Boylen, J. Thomas, H. Kershaw, F. Smith, J. Lomas (captain),
T.H. Newbould, W. Jukes, J. Bartholomew, W. Ward; second row: W. Dell
(visitor), F. Webster, W. Batten, Bert Jenkins, J.H. Houghton (manager),
J. Clifford (manager), A.E. Avery, J. Riley, J. Davis, D. Murray (trainer);
front: J. Sharrock, F. Young, Chic Jenkins, F. Farrar.

A CIP catalogue record for this book is available from the British Library.

First published in Great Britain in May 2010 by:
London League Publications Ltd, P.O. Box 10441, London E14 8WR

ISBN: 978-1903659-51-9

Cover design by: Stephen McCarthy Graphic Design
                    46, Clarence Road, London N15 5BB

Layout: Peter Lush

Printed and bound by: MPG Books Group, Bodmin and King's Lynn

Foreword: They were treated like kings

At the first sound of 1907's revolutionary trumpet – the news that 'professional rugby' was coming to Australia and New Zealand under the 13-a-side game of the Northern Union – there was one golden bullet that caught the eyes and ears of every Antipodean football player and supporter.

It was the news that, not only would we be sending our first national rugby teams to England, but that a party of real English rugby footballers would be coming here, to visit our shores, and test themselves on our fields against us!

For decades we had enjoyed in our thousands watching on as our cricketers battled against the touring teams from England. When our cricketers returned the favour with visits to England, we waited patiently for English newspapers to arrive here on mail ships, with six-week-old news of our boys triumphs and troubles with the bat and ball.

We knew a fair bit about rugby in England too – no one ever forgot the 1888 British team. Seven years before 'The Great Split' from rugby union, these first visitors to our shores lived long in our memories. The mighty backbone of the 1888 team were "hardy north countrymen". Brawny, thick-set, they were seemingly born to play the rugby game. Off the field they were genial, but still more than lively spirited. They were like us, and immensely popular for it.

Two-thirds of the 21-man squad in 1888 came from Yorkshire, Lancashire and Cheshire – from now famous clubs and well-familiar town names to any Antipodean rugby league fan, including Swinton, Batley, Salford, Halifax, Runcorn, Dewsbury and Rochdale.

While further tours under the RFU banner came here in 1899 and 1904, these two teams were different – they didn't have the "real rugby men" from the north, the home of "the best rugby material in England". And we knew it.

The prospect of a visit from a 'real' British team under professional rugby was a great fillip for the pioneers of the code in Australia and New Zealand.

Where some may have faltered, despaired at the rumours of impending doom or given up in the tough early going of 1907 to 1909, the knowledge that a promise had been made by the Northern Union to send a representative team gave us all great heart.

Significantly, the decision in mid-1909 for 14 current rugby union Wallabies to cross to rugby league dealt the amateur code a near-fatal blow. It was the news, though, that the 1910 visit of the Northern Union team was practically assured that swayed many of those Wallabies to change allegiance to the 13-man code.

In a sense, the visit of the 1910 Lions and the immense crowds they drew to games in Australia was more akin to a three-months long victory celebration, rather than the battle-changing mortar-blows of a protracted war.

The rugby war in Australia was ostensibly over before the 1910 Lions arrived. The hope and promise of their visit had already fuelled the initial rebellion and ultimately turned the Wallabies and the tide.

That the 1910 tourists didn't fail to meet expectations, sent rugby league sky-rocketing in popularity.

The tourists left for home firmly in the knowledge that they had placed rugby league as the premier football code in NSW and Queensland – it has held this place of pre-eminence, built on the 1910 Lions, ever since.

The importance of the 1910 Lions to the game of rugby league can never be understated – that's why their story needs to be told and recognised.

They forged the test tour tradition against the Kangaroos – for the Ashes – and the Kiwis that would serve international rugby league so well through the 20th century. It's hard to imagine what would have become of the code in Australia and New Zealand, and indeed in England, had the regular exchanging of tours not become so integral to the game. It was that international appeal that swayed us from looking inwards and opting to take up Melbourne's Victorian rules game.

The first immortal of the game in Australia, Dally Messenger, said of the 1910 Lions, "They were treated like kings".

So they were, and so they should always be.

Sean Fagan

Sean Fagan has done ground-breaking work on the early days of both rugby codes in Australia and New Zealand. Recent books include *The Rugby Rebellion* and *The Master – The life and times of Dally Messenger* (with Dally Messenger III)

Bibliography

Code XIII, (Editor Trevor Delaney) James Leytham's personal diary of the tour
The History of Rugby League Football by Keith Macklin
History of Rugby League series by Irvin Saxton
The Kiwis – A history of NZ Rugby League by John Coffey and Bernie Wood
The New Zealand Rugby League Annual 1933
The Northern Union minutes book for the period
The Northern Union 1910 Tour Brochure
Thrum Hall Greats by Andrew Hardcastle
100 Greats Huddersfield RLFC by David Gronow
100 Greats Salford Rugby League club by Graham Morris
Rugby League in Manchester by Graham Morris
The Rugby Rebellion by Sean Fagan
Newspapers: *Athletic News Weekly, Auckland Star, Brisbane Courier, Yorkshire Post, Lancaster Guardian, Morning Post* (London), *New Zealand Herald, Otago Witness, Sydney Morning Herald, The Colonist* (New Zealand), *The Evening Post* (Wellington New Zealand), *The Referee* (Australia), *The Sydney Mail, The Sydney Sportsman, The Sydney Sun, The Sydney Telegraph, The Wanganui Herald, New Zealand Freelance.*

James Lomas – the first Lions captain

My name is Robin James Lomas Dellar and I am a grandson of James Lomas the famous rugby league international of the early 1900s. I have a younger brother, Brian Euan Lomas Dellar who is known as Bunny. Our mother Evelyn was one of four daughters born to Annie and James. After marriage she settled in the London area. Two of her sisters Madge and Olive settled in Belfast, while Annie remained in Salford.

James Lomas was born in 1880 at Maryport, Cumberland and was one of three children, the others were girls. His father also named James Lomas was a boot and shoemaker by trade at Maryport, and in his youth was a wrestler of some repute. His wife had four children by a previous marriage, two boys and two girls.

One of the boys was named Tom Smith, who played professional football for both Preston North End and Tottenham Hotspur. While with Tottenham, Smith won an FA Cup winners' medal in 1901 and scored the second goal in a 3–1 victory against Sheffield United.

In his prime he was only 5 feet 7 inches tall, but weighed 13 stones and was renowned for his physical prowess and often competed in professional sprinting. He played rugby league for Maryport, Bramley, Salford, Oldham, York and Wakefield, but it was at Salford that he became famous. As captain for 10 years he was the leading points scorer in every season, and was awarded the honour of captaining the first Northern Union side to tour Australia and New Zealand in 1910. He was the very first £100 transfer player, and later first £300 transfer.

Following his retirement he rejoined his old club Salford to help out during the First World War in 1917, when aged 37, he played three games. He took over as reserve team coach in 1922, and was asked to play again in 1923 turning out six times in February and March, and twice more in September at the great age of 43.

During the Second World War my mother, Bunny and I stayed with my grandparents for a short time at Byron Street in Salford. They were a quiet unassuming couple giving no signs of earlier fame and achievements. Mother told us that James had offers of business opportunities in his retirement but was reluctant to take the challenge and was content to find work at the local Salford docks. He was still working at the age of 72 when interviewed by the local press, where it was noted that he still possessed fitness greater than many men some 20 years younger. During his time at the docks his rugby skills were again put to the test, when he was forced to fend off a swinging bale, saving a man's life.

James took great interest when Bunny, on leaving school, signed professional terms with Chelsea Football Club. He gained England youth international honours, but never made the first team. He then spent many years playing in the semi-professional Southern League.

James Lomas died in hospital on 11 February 1960, and was honoured on the following Saturday at the Willows by a minute's silence, with both teams wearing black armbands.

Robin Dellar

Acknowledgements

Any book that deals with an historical subject is going to tax any writer and this one is no exception. Consequently, a great many people have had an input into the production of this book and therefore deserve to be thanked. If I have inadvertently forgotten to mention someone I ask their forgiveness and hope they will put it down to the failing memory caused by age.

I would like to thank Sean Fagan the Australian rugby historian for information on the Australian perspectives in 1910; David Middleton from League Information and the staff of the reference library of New South Wales in Sydney. Similarly from New Zealand, my thanks must go to John Coffey and Bernie Wood, the New Zealand rugby league historians, for their help on the New Zealand perspective, Don Henderson from the New Zealand Rugby League Kiwis Association, and Yvonne Chisholm. All have freely offered information, particularly on Albert Baskerville and events in Rotorua.

In Great Britain, I must thank Professor Tony Collins, the RFL's archivist; Hilary Haigh and the staff at the University of Huddersfield library, Brian Walker and Mick Harrop of the Oldham RL Heritage Trust and the 'Roughyeds'; David Gronow of the Huddersfield Past Players' Association; Graham Morris; Rob Dellar; John Edwards, Fred Jackson, Bill Dalton; Richard Bailey of the Rugby League Collectors Federation; Tony Holmes; Neil Dowson; and finally Dave Parker at *League Weekly* for publicising my requests for information about the tour.

There is one person who deserves special mention and that is Peter Sullivan who took photographs which were 100 years old and digitally cleaned them up to such a state that they became publishable. Without his efforts the book would be all the poorer. Thanks to Stephen McCarthy for designing the cover, Peter Lush for layout, Michael O'Hare for proofreading and the staff of MPG Biddles for printing it.

Last, but by no means least, thank you to my wife Janet for once more reading the text and offering advice and ideas.

Tom Mather
December 2009

The Leytham Diary

I made great efforts to locate the grandson of James Leytham to ask permission to use the diary, sadly without success. I do hope that he would be pleased with the resulting efforts. Extracts from his diary are reproduced as he wrote it; the only changes made are by the author with regard to the spelling and so on.

Maori

It should be noted that just a few years ago it was pointed out by Maori authorities in New Zealand to all the media that there is no plural in the Maori language. Therefore all references made in the past to Maoris were incorrect. Consequently, in this book, all plural references made have been changed to Maori.

Best in the Northern Union

These tourists do not seem to have had a nickname – not even 'pioneers'. 'Best in the Northern Union' was a popular phrase before the First World War in the north of England to indicate quality, and seemed appropriate as a title for this book.

Some of the photographs in this book are not of the high quality London League Publications Ltd usually strive to achieve. This is because of the age of the photographs.

Contents

1.	Beyond three counties	1
2.	Going on tour	15
3.	Life on the ocean waves	31
4.	Let the games commence	39
5.	The Ashes	63
6.	Australasia	83
7.	The land of the long white cloud	97
8.	Homeward bound	121

Appendices

1. The tourists	128
2. Statistics and records	143
3. Baskerville or Baskiville?	145

The cover of the tour handbook.

1. Beyond three counties

It was the defining moment of the first ever tour to Australia by the Northern Union. The first test had been won by the tourists in Sydney, but here in Brisbane they faced a much tougher struggle. They were down to 12 men, George Ruddick having been sent off for rough play. True, the visitors were winning, but with the score 19–11 were far from safe, particularly as the great Dally Messenger was starting to run the show as the game was entering the final stages and the Lions were tiring.

Not for the first time the superior numbers of the Australian pack were made to tell and yet another ball was heeled out on their side. Messenger took the ball on the halfway line and, with electrifying speed, cut through the tiring British defence. He was only halted by a great tackle by the full-back Sharrock, yards from the tryline. Somehow the British forwards got back, began scrummaging for the ball and cleared their line, only for the Australian backs to launch another attack. This again was halted yards from the line and tired British bodies once more somehow managed to win the ball. This time instead of kicking to clear his line, Billy Jukes scooped up the ball and broke through a couple of would-be tacklers. As he broke clear, on his shoulder was the wingman James Leytham who called for and got the ball. It was then a 90-yard foot race between him and the Australian Dugald McGregor. Leytham won, planted the ball down over the line for his fourth try and, more importantly, clinched the second test and with it the Ashes for the tourists.

*****

In the history of any sport there are defining moments like Leytham's. There are moments or events which dictate how the sport itself will progress and there are moments within games that decide which team or individual will win and which will lose.

Rugby league, throughout its chequered history, has seen defining moments and events, and landmark decisions being made. One of the most important moments in the sport's history came 100 years ago, in 1910. The Northern Union's governing body decided to send a team to tour Australia and New Zealand. Today such trips are commonplace, but in 1910 it was a very brave decision indeed. That tour, the first undertaken by the Northern Union, was to contain defining moments, not just for the game in Great Britain, but also in Australia and New Zealand.

It was a tour that was to see the first rugby league Ashes series in Australia; rugby league established as the leading football code in New South Wales and Queensland and the game make progress in New Zealand. There were moments of great controversy and at least one major missed opportunity.

That first tour came at the culmination of a three-year period in the sport's history that had established the game in England and on the international stage. It would not be exaggerating to say that the period from 1907 to 1910 saved the game from sinking into oblivion or even returning to rugby union. Everything in the garden had appeared to be so rosy just 15 years or so prior to the 1910 tour.

The initial period, following the breakaway in 1895, was one of seemingly continuous success. Many clubs in the north joined the fledgling Northern Union. The senior clubs in Lancashire and Yorkshire, had despaired of winning the battle over 'broken time' with the Rugby Union and would not give up the authority they had wrung from their respective county unions over promotion and relegation to the leagues which they effectively ran. They had resigned from the Rugby Union and formed the Northern Union. One effect of this was that junior clubs in the region following suit, not always because they wanted to, but because they had to in order to survive financially. This argument was put forward by the author and Michael Latham in their book *The Rugby League Myth* in 1993.

After the initial successes that followed the breakaway, familiarity bred contempt, particularly with the fans. They began to make their feelings known by voting with their feet, as they had done prior to the breakaway. They were paying good money and wanted to be entertained, and were not satisfied just with club fare. To satisfy this appetite for a higher level of competitive rugby the authorities had introduced a County Championship, involving Lancashire, Yorkshire and Cheshire. Rugby union had run a county championship, which prior to 1895 was dominated by Yorkshire and Lancashire.

In the Northern Union's second season, in 1896–97, they introduced the Challenge Cup competition. Both measures were aimed at stimulating interest, both for spectators and for players aspiring to win a county cap or Challenge Cup medal.

The initial surge of enthusiasm that had driven the game forward waned. There was an upsurge in the popularity of association football that was eating into the rugby league club's fan base. By the 1902–03 season things were so bad that the Yorkshire and Lancashire Senior competitions were abandoned and the league was divided into First and Second Divisions. This was caused mainly by the fall in the number of professional clubs in membership from 41 to 36. Some of the fringe clubs were finding professionalism hard to sustain and they succumbed through lack of finance. It was also in this season that the first suggestions were made about reducing the number of players on the pitch. There were two reasons for this. One was to make the game more attractive to supporters – in some games there were as many as 120 scrums – and fewer players on the field could lead to more open and attractive rugby. The second was to reduce the financial outgoings of the clubs on their players.

At the Northern Union AGM in July 1903, it was proposed to reduce the number of players in a team from 15 to 12. There was a feeling that something needed to be done to make the game more attractive. If they did not, the fear was that the fast-growing association game would "oust it in popular favour."

As the two-thirds majority required under the rules was not obtained, the motion was not carried. No action was taken and the 1903–04 season maintained the status quo. It was a situation which could not continue if the sport was to survive. The committee did take some action, but decided to limit it to representative games rather than league and cup games. The following season the County Championship was played with 12 men in each team. This was an experiment to assess the viability of playing the game with only five forwards, instead of eight. The first international match was organised along similar lines. England played the Other Nationalities. The match was played at Wigan on 5 April, the original fixture falling victim to the frost in early January. Again the teams consisted of 12 players, with only five forwards making up the pack. The Other Nationalities team was mainly made up of Welsh players. Later the fixture would become an international match between England and Wales.

Despite this, the game was still in decline and the financial problems clubs faced led to more resignations from the league. In 1903–04 there were 35 clubs, but in 1904–05 only 32. The two divisions could not be sustained and so was abolished. The 31 senior clubs instigated a ridiculous situation for the 1905–06 season, whereby they would decide their own fixture lists, and any club unable to obtain more than 10 first class fixtures would be discarded from the league.

Things were getting so bad that in October 1905 Hull FC submitted a resolution, that the Northern Union rejoin the Rugby Union. This was rejected and, at the AGM in 1906, a number of proposals were put forward to reduce the number of players on the field. Some clubs favoured 12, others 13 and others 14. Eventually, the proposal to reduce the number of players in a team to 13 was passed by a vote of 43 to 18. The game was attempting to combat the popularity of association football by this move, but its salvation lay in something on the other side of the world that would generate a monumental change in the game, over a short period of time.

Since 1895, the new code had realised it needed to change the rules to make the sport more attractive to watch. In 1897, scoring had been standardised and line-outs abolished. The key change came in 1906 when, along with the change to 13-a-side, the play-the-ball was introduced after a tackle. This was, and still remains, the fundamental difference between rugby league and rugby union. In 1908, the object of the game became to score tries and goals, rather than just goals. In 1909 the rule regarding the ball going into touch was changed. The next major change was the abolition of unlimited tackles in the 1966.

In New Zealand a young postal worker by the name of Albert Baskerville had developed a reputation on the rugby field as a winger who was both big and quick, assets as important then as they are today. In 1906 Baskerville was played for the Oriental club in Wellington. Popular folklore is that one of his colleagues at the Post Office, while having a coughing fit dropped a copy of the *Athletic News Weekly*, an English newspaper he was reading. Baskerville picked it up and read that a Northern Union game in Bradford had attracted a large crowd, maybe the 27,000 that saw the local team play Halifax in the Challenge Cup. He saw the opportunities for making a financial killing by organising a tour of New Zealanders to play the professional game in the north of England.

The 1905 tour of Great Britain by the New Zealand All Blacks Rugby Union team had been financially successful, but the £12,000 tour profits had gone straight into the coffers of the New Zealand Rugby Union. Many of those players whose efforts on the field had raised that money had returned from the tour both saddened and disillusioned. Saddened because they had not been able to play against the crack clubs in Lancashire and Yorkshire – and so felt they had not played or beaten the best English teams, and disillusioned by the way they had been treated by the New Zealand Rugby Union.

By January 1907, Baskerville had begun secret correspondence with the Northern Union secretary, Joseph Platt. There was only one thing on the agenda, a tour by a New Zealand team to England. He wanted to know if such a tour was viable or not, would the Northern Union accept a tour and if he could obtain financial guarantees from the Northern Union. He estimated that to finance such a tour would take around £3,000 and he wanted the clubs or the NU to guarantee this sum. By March, 1907 the matters had been resolved, the £3,000 was guaranteed by the Northern Union, and the tourists would receive 70 per cent of all gate receipts at matches played.

All that was needed now was to get the Northern Union clubs to agree and keep the whole affair secret from the New Zealand Rugby Union until Baskerville had got his tourists signed up and on board ship. The clubs in Lancashire and Yorkshire quickly realised the value of such a tour. They were not really concerned about the international game as such, but rather the opportunity of a bumper gate against the tourists. A bumper gate meant high receipts. They also felt that such matches would generate interest among supporters.

However, Baskerville needed to keep his plans quiet, a massive feat given that he had to approach players about the possibility of touring England as professionals, and hope they would keep their own counsel. It was quite an undertaking, but he managed it. The first inkling of such a tour did not hit the media in New Zealand until the beginning of May. On 8 May 1907, the *Evening Post* in Wellington published a short piece which read:

Proposed team for England
Napier 7 May
The Hawkes Bay Rugby Union at its meeting tonight passed a resolution: 'That this union views with disapproval the movement now being made to send a professional team of footballers to England, and urges the New Zealand Rugby Union to do its utmost to kill the proposal, as in the opinion of this union it is likely to have a very damaging effect upon amateur rugby football in the future.'

It is not clear how or where the Hawkes Bay RU got the information from. Given the number of people involved, maybe it was inevitable that rumours would start to circulate within the game and they would be picked up by the rugby union officials.

One of the conditions for touring was that each player had to raise £50 prior to being accepted. It was this fact that Baskerville used to counter the arguments that the players were professionals. He said that the players were paying to play the game and would take a share of any profits the tour made. This was the way in which privately organised cricket tours had been organised in the past and he saw no difference in his plans.

So the cat was out of the bag in New Zealand. However, it did not stop Baskerville continuing the process of selecting players for the tour. He would not have been helped by the news coming from London, just a few days later. It was reported in Wellington in the *Evening Post* on 11 May that: "[There was an] announcement from London that there is a probability of a team of professional 'All Blacks' making a trip to England to play the Northern Union representatives..." Baskerville must not have been pleased to read that in the local paper because he was still negotiating in secret with players. Throughout the rest of May, the papers were full of rumour and innuendo regarding the proposed tour and its professional nature. As the month progressed, more and more rumours and half-truths, claims and counter-claims came to the fore, with rugby writers and supporters reporting hearsay as fact. More provincial rugby union bodies passed resolutions condemning the notion of a professional tour, even though officially they had no knowledge of such a tour. They were also scurrying about trying to find out whatever they could about the plans and who was behind them.

It was not until 28 May that the tour was officially acknowledged by the New Zealand Rugby Union. For the previous three weeks they had been busy behind the scenes trying to find any information. At the same time they were trying to get all players to sign a declaration of amateur status in an attempt to thwart any professional tour. This was causing a great deal of upset among players and supporters alike, not all of whom were opposed to the tour. The New Zealand rugby union authorities demanded players sign their declaration or face not being selected for any representative side. Many players took exception to being asked to sign such a declaration, resenting that they were being doubted over their amateur status and that their word was not enough.

The newspapers were still desperately trying to find out all they could about the proposed tour and on 27 May the *Evening Post* published an article under the headline:

6

'All Black' Professional Scheme

A representative of the *Post* has been informed on good authority that the 'All Black' team of rugby footballers, which is going Home [i.e. England] to play the English Northern Union clubs, is not being organised by a speculative syndicate, as has been reported in various quarters. The players are financing themselves, although they have been offered outside financial assistance if it is required.

It was probably this article that prompted the New Zealand rugby union authorities to act as they did the following day. It is interesting that other people were prepared to offer financial help to Baskerville should he have required it. Just who those people were is not known, but they must have been astute enough to realise such a venture was potentially very profitable, and they were right. The *Evening Post* carried a larger article on 28 May.

The 'All Black' professionals

The New Zealand Rugby Union, through its management committee, has at last, after negotiations that have been going on between New Zealand and the North of England for 12 months, obtained the name of one of the parties interested in the professional movement. The gentleman in question is a well-known Wellington player who has taken part in senior championship matches for several years past.

The New Zealand Union drafted a letter, which it sent to the player in question. He played his last amateur game on the Saturday, and then resigned as an amateur player. The New Zealand Union in its letter asked him to attend a special meeting of the union. As he did not attend, the correspondence below was read out.

25 May 1907
Mr A.H. Baskiville,
Dear Sir,
This union has reason to believe that you have information upon the proposed tour of professional footballers to England, and by instruction I summon you to meet the management committee of the union in my office at Brown's Building, Johnson Street on Monday next 27th... at 8pm.
Yours faithfully
J.D. Avery (Secretary).

The reply was:

27 May 1907
The Secretary
N.Z. Rugby Union
Sir,
Your union will no doubt gain all the information that I have regarding the proposed tour of "All Black" professional footballers to England from the daily newspapers in the course of a few weeks. Until then I am bound not to divulge it. As I severed my connection with the Oriental Football Club on the 25th inst., and I am also leaving the Postal Department, be good enough in future to post all communications to me at the above address. I am etc...
A. H. Baskiville
Hon. Secretary NZ Rugby Football Club.

The NZRU management committee passed the following resolution:
"That A. H. Baskiville be dealt with under rule 2 sub section (1) clause (1), under the rules as to professionalism, and that all unions be asked to prevent him from entering football grounds under their control."

The clause in the rules referred to included among acts of professionalism the following: "Any individual refusing to give evidence or otherwise assisting in carrying out these rules when requested by the union to do so."

The newspaper also reported that the people involved in the proposed tour would not comment any further.

It was also reported that the council of the New South Wales Rugby Union passed the following resolution on 27 May: "That this council conveys to the New Zealand Rugby Union its hearty appreciation of the action taken in reference to the suggested visit of a professional team to England, being of opinion that such action is in the best interests of the game."

This is the first time this correspondence has seen the light of day since 1907. On 26 March 1907, the Northern Union Committee in England had a formal proposal from New Zealand. The committee agreed to hold more meetings in order to consider other ways of guaranteeing the money requested. They decided to circulate the clubs for their views. Almost all the clubs, as mentioned earlier, recognised the value of a tour and applied for a fixture against the tourists. So it was that the so-called 'All-Gold' tour came into being.

It seems strange that this first ever tour is referred to as the 'All-Golds' tour and this is now regarded as a term of endearment. In fact, it was not always known by that name. It was very rarely referred to as the All-Golds tour while it was going on. The earliest reference found to the tour and the suggestion that the players were only playing for the money, hence All-Golds, was the cartoon by Stuart Reid published in the *Otago Witness* on 5 June 1907. He suggested that the New Zealand shirt badge of a silver fern and actuarial table is replaced by an Pounds, Shillings and Pence sign. On the top of the badge is the Latin phrase Aurum Cupidimus which literally translated means 'love of gold', or 'seeker of gold', hence All-Golds. Also on his All Black shirt are the letters PRO, presumably short for professional.

The first written reference to the term All-Gold was in the *Sydney Morning Herald* on 7 August 1907 when the tourists arrived in Australia on the way to England and was unearthed by Australian historian Sean Fagan. More often at that time the tourists were referred to as the 'professional All-Blacks' or the New Zealand Northern Union team. That description was also used by the Northern Union when describing test matches against the tourists and in their 1910 tour brochure.

There can be no doubt that the All-Golds tour helped save the game in Great Britain. Baskerville, once he had received official approval from England, set about the task with relish. There was a small article in the *Evening Post* of 1 August which provides an insight into the way Baskerville's mind worked and just how far-sighted he really was. The article said that Baskerville had been appointed as manager for the tour but it is the fact that he hoped to play matches in both France and America which is fascinating.

The article read: "The professional Rugby team will play a match in Paris on its way to England, and an invitation had been accepted to play in California on the return to the colony. The team will be known as the 'All Blacks' wearing the same costume as the former New Zealand [union] team. No less than 160 applications were received for places on the team. The selected members will assemble in Sydney, where three matches will be played, to be followed probably by others in Melbourne and Adelaide. Mr J.C. Gleeson has been appointed playing manager."

Sadly, the plans to play in Victoria, and the Paris and American parts of the tour, never materialised, but the ideas were in Baskerville's head to do this at some stage. There was no mention of the All-Gold title for the tourists. It was not something the press really ever picked up on.

On 13 September the *Morning Post* in London carried an interview with Cecil Wray Palliser, the Agent-General for New Zealand. He did not pull his punches when expressing his views on the proposed tour. This is not surprising as well as being the Agent-General (a diplomatic representative of a colonial government in London) he was also the New Zealand Rugby Union representative to the Rugby Union in London. He said: "I want to make it quite plain that, whatever the side from New Zealand to play the Northern Union clubs, it will not in the slightest degree represent either the Rugby Union Football of New Zealand or the sporting community of the colony...

"Everything is being done to hoodwink the public in England, even to the extent of sending home results of matches between the side that is coming and others in Australia.

"Anyone can get up a side and call it anything that is desired. You could pick up a side anywhere from the colonies and endow it with any colonial name. Even now we may be pursuing a phantom team. There is no news of its sailing from New Zealand. This secrecy may be part of the plan to act as a make-believe to Northern Union supporters.

"These Northern Union clubs are quite strong in their particular game and if this mythical side does eventually materialise it will be beaten to pieces or only allowed to win on sufferance."

He was equally scathing in his views of the Northern Union, even though it was now in its 13th season and seemingly well entrenched into the sporting psychic of the north of England. He continued: "The Northern Union in the courage of despair generated by the inroads in its domain by professional Association [football] and by the spirit of real rugby, was bound to make some kind of sensation to sure itself.

"We are a third of the way through September. The Northern Union has neither divulged its wonderful list of players, nor mentioned the good ship on which the side sails. Is it a phantom team?"

It was a disgraceful outburst, particularly from a government official, but does show the intense dislike the Northern Union had engendered in rugby union officialdom. Association football, it would seem, even with its professionals, was acceptable to Wray Palliser, as was cricket which also accepted professionals playing alongside amateurs. Professional rugby however, was not "real rugby". Given that Wray Palliser had written to the New Zealand Rugby Union back in May, reported in the New Zealand press, asking for details of the proposed tour and in his letter referred to the great excitement the tour was generating in the North of England, there can be no doubt that he was fully aware of the touring team, yet chose to deny its very existence.

At worst it must be said that he would have been fully informed that the professionals had set off to Australia and were then to sail for England. Wray Palliser chose to ignore such facts. He even cast doubts about the match reports published by the Wellington *Evening Post,* suggesting they too were a hoax. Yet the *Morning Post* in London did not challenge him on this point. It appears that Wray Palliser was making a deliberate attempt to destabilise the tour before it began and to do so by whatever means possible.

It was an outburst that the Northern Union could not allow to go unanswered. While the *Morning Post* was unlikely to give them the right of reply, the NU secretary, Joseph Platt, did issue a statement the following day: "I announced over a week ago that the team sailed on August 24 in the SS Ortona which is due at Naples on September 29. An overland journey of 36 hours will then be made.

"The team has not been disclosed because this was an agreement with the promoter Mr Baskerville, and his permission was awaited."

It was a sordid episode and highlighted the steps rugby union was prepared to take in order to discredit Baskerville and his professional team. It was well known that the team was on its way. The New Zealand Rugby Union had banned them for life but allowed Wray Palliser, their representative, to make such misleading statements to the *Morning Post*. None of this stopped the tourists arriving in England.

Perhaps as a follow up to his announcement in reply to Wray Palliser's outburst, Platt released a letter he had received from Baskerville. He arranged for it to be published in the *Yorkshire Post* on 24 September, barely a week before the tourists were due to arrive. In the letter Baskerville wrote of events in Sydney following the three matches the New Zealand tourists had played there.

The letter said: "The formation of rugby league in Sydney has been a great sensation... The intention is not to pay actual wages but to pay broken time, to pay all out-of-pocket expenses when away from home and to provide an ample insurance scheme in case of accident... Players connected with the rebel league who had been threatened with a 'loss of billet' [a loss of their job] would be looked after."

At an official reception for the tourists, when they arrived at the end of September, Joseph Platt informed the gathered throng, that a letter had been received from James (J.J.) Giltinan. Giltinan had given the letter to Baskerville prior to him leaving Australia and asked that he deliver it by hand to Platt. In the letter he requested 50 copies of the Northern Union rulebook. Giltinan was the secretary of the newly formed New South Wales Rugby Football League. He also suggested in his letter that a tour should be organised involving Australia. He was certainly not slow to put forward his own case.

Once again Platt arranged for Giltinan's letter to be published in the *Yorkshire Post* on 2 October and shows evidence of his intentions and ideas: "Perhaps it is a bit premature to ask you to invite our League to play your Union a series of matches in your country but this would assist League in New South Wales." "A bit premature" was something of an understatement from Giltinan, the league he talks of did not even exist except in his mind and those of a couple of others in Sydney. There was, however, method in his approach as he used the possibility of a professional tour to England in 1908 as a carrot to dangle before the players in Sydney. If they wanted to make the tour they needed to be playing Northern Union rugby. They could not do so unless they formed Northern Union clubs – and 1908 saw the start of the first league competition in Sydney.

The 1908 New Zealand tourists. Back: R. Wynward, A. Lile, D. Gilchrist, E. Tyne, C. Dunning, W. Tyler, Middle: A.H. Baskerville, C.J. Pearce, A.F. Kelly, J. A. Lavery, D.D. Fraser, A. Callam, C.A. Byrne, W.T.Wynward, J.H. Smith, Hodgson (non player), H.S. Turtill; front: W. Johnston, William Trevarthen, H.H. Messenger, C.E. Wrigley, G.W. Smith, H.R. Wright, C.D. McGregor, W. Mackrell, Harold Rowe, L.B. Todd, T. Cross.

So, even as the All-Golds were touring Great Britain, and doing so very successfully, the British clubs were in favour of an Australian team coming the following season. They would have felt such a tour would match the interest and success generated by the New Zealanders. International Northern Union rugby was now a reality and the crowds were flocking to watch it. The future of the game seemed secure.

The New Zealand team arrived in England on 30 September, docking in Folkestone. Over the next four-and-a-half months they played 35 games, losing 14 of them, and more importantly winning two of the three test matches in Great Britain, not bad for a team that supposedly did not even exist. Sadly there is no record of Wray Palliser's views of the achievements of his countrymen. The New Zealand tourists had allowed the game in Great Britain to turn the corner; events over the next two seasons would see it stand tall and proud for the first time since immediately after the breakaway.

The game that had been in danger of fading away, due in no small part to the insular nature of its organisation, had been thrown a lifeline. As the Northern Union was waving goodbye to the New Zealand tourists it was preparing to welcome the Australian touring party and James Giltinan, the following season. On 27 September 1908, almost a year to the day after the All-Golds had come to Britain, the first Kangaroos arrived. Their tour was not to be as successful, either on the field, or from a spectator point of view.

The tour was a financial disaster and was badly affected by poor weather. However, as 1908 drew to a close, the first seeds were sewn for a possible tour by the Union down under, when the NU committee agreed to consider it. That it was going to happen was due solely to the actions of one man, Albert Baskerville, who had sadly died in Australia when the team stopped there on the way home. He alone had stirred up the Northern Union and the game in three countries. This international development went a long way toward securing the future of rugby league. It was the 1910 tour that would establish rugby league as the major game in Australia and a strong foothold for the game in New Zealand. These tours by the New Zealanders and then the Australians to Great Britain defined the path the game was to follow over the next few years, which played a major part in securing its future, as the possibility of international competition was now there for players and supporters, as it was in rugby union and association football.

2. Going on tour

The first official record of the Northern Union considering the possibility of a tour to Australia and New Zealand was in the management committee minutes of 28 December 1908. There can be little doubt that the committee was responding to the prompting and cajoling of James Giltinan, who was in Great Britain touring with the Australians. He knew full well that he needed such a tour if the league in Sydney was to develop further. If they were to combat the ongoing opposition from rugby union, Giltinan needed something to convince more players to switch to the rugby league code, a visit by the Northern Union team would go a long way towards achieving that goal. It was true that the new domestic league had been reasonably successful but more was needed if the progress was to continue. The NU Council meeting minutes of that date recorded: "The question of a visit to Australia and New Zealand was under consideration and after some discussion it was decided to defer the question pending the cable to be sent to the secretary of the New Zealand Union asking whether they were sufficiently organised to accept a visit by the Northern Union team for next season."

The cable to New Zealand was duly dispatched by Joseph Platt, who did not have long to wait for the reply. When the committee met on 12 January 1909 a reply had been received from down under. Sadly it was a negative response. Platt reported the contents of the cable he had received: "Only established a short time, not sufficient to warrant a visit; writing."

Daniel Fraser, the secretary of the New Zealand Rugby League, did write to the NU and what he said would not have inspired confidence that a tour would be successful. In an interview in the *Otago Witness* on 13 January 1910 Fraser told the reporter that he would not make terms with the tourists until they were in Australia.

He went on to tell the reporter that in his letter to Joseph Platt he had expressed the opinion that the gates the tourists would attract both in Australia and New Zealand would be too small to warrant them coming. He continued with the theme that the people in New Zealand were "tired" of rugby at the present time. He ended the interview by saying that if the tour to Australia did go ahead, the Australians wanted a New Zealand team to go to Sydney and take part in a tournament with Australia and England. It seems that the idea of a Tri-

Nations competition was suggested around 100 years ago, showing that there really is nothing new in the game.

Given this news the consensus was that it would be unwise to send a team to New Zealand next year. However, the committee was not shutting the door; they decided that they would be prepared to consider an invitation for the following season. Australia was a different matter; a tour sub-committee was set up to establish a dialogue with the Australian executive presently in the country, with the aim of establishing terms which would form the basis on which all future tours should be financed.

The only other item for discussion by the committee was an application it had received from Mr P.T. Moko. He had requested that the Northern Union be prepared to accept a visit from a Maori team during the 1909–10 season. It was felt that while the British were trying to organise their own first tour, it would not be an opportune time to also be involved in planning and organising a Maori tour to Britain. Mr Moko sadly received a negative response.

The Australian tourists set off for home on 10 March 1909. The tour had been fraught with difficulties right from the beginning. On arrival the Australians were met with a strike by the cotton mill workers in Lancashire. Consequently, perhaps the workers perhaps had little money to spend on watching them play.

It is possible to judge the mood of the party. Four of the party were not returning having signed for Northern Union clubs in England and the tour financially had been a flop. The financial returns had been so bad that the Northern Union had to pay passage home for the tourists. The tour captain was full of praise for the hospitality the players had received, but upset by the bad weather that had dogged the tour. He was mindful that injuries to players had badly affected results but felt they had all adapted quickly to the weather, the likes of which many of them had not experienced before. Out of 45 matches played, the tourists won 17 and drew six. The kangaroo which was their mascot throughout the tour died the day before they were to leave, which seemed to symbolise their experiences on tour.

Writing much later, Dally Messenger revealed that finances were so bad that the Northern Union gave every player £1 to allow them to buy provisions while on board ship. He also revealed that at one point during the tour, when finances were particularly poor, results and consequently gate receipts were equally bad. This, in turn, had led to the morale of the players being at rock bottom. James Giltinan had hired a large house in Southport and staffed it for the tour party out of his own pocket. Messenger stated that morale bucked up no end as a result of the time spent in Southport. He said that the team felt more together having their own cook and housekeeper with them rather than being in cold and impersonal hotel rooms.

Giltinan, supported by the Northern Union, insisted on charging one shilling admission for their games. The standard club game admission was only sixpence. Many supporters felt the fare served up by the Australians was not of the same calibre as that of the New Zealanders the year before and did not warrant spending an extra sixpence to see. Equally the Northern Union, in attempting to spread the word about their game, arranged for matches to be played up and down the land. Two of the tests were played at Newcastle and London, with little thought of what other sporting events would be held in competition with their matches which could detract from the gate.

But with the tourists now departed and the season coming to an end, officials were free to apply their time and energy to preparing for the tour the Northern Union was to undertake. Yet, as the season concluded, a bombshell was dropped on the committee. A letter arrived from the New South Wales Rugby League.

James Giltinan was still at sea on the way home when this letter arrived on Joseph Platt's desk. While he had been in England with the tourists there had been growing unrest in the New South Wales Rugby League Committee. This unrest was first hinted at by the newspapers who suggested that Giltinan, Henry (Harry) Hoyle and Victor Trumper were guilty of secrecy, acting alone and withholding information on the league's accounts from the committee. In effect, it was alleged that they acted as if they owned the league, which is exactly what they probably thought and – in essence – did.

Rumours were also circulating that Hoyle was refusing all attempts by the committee to form a management and financial sub-committee for the league. He probably felt that skeletons which were safely locked away would start popping out of the cupboard. The Australian newspapers had targeted Giltinan, saying that he 'edited' correspondence to 'suit his own ideas'. Letters were mislaid or disappeared, it was claimed, if the content did not meet with his approval. In modern parlance, Giltinan was being a little economical with the truth. Perhaps Hoyle had been trying to hold back the torrent until Giltinan arrived back in Australia and was able to give him some support and – he hoped – answers to the rest of the committee.

At the Annual General Meeting in March 1909 no accounts were forthcoming. This discrepancy was questioned by Alexander Knox who asked that accounts be produced and demanded to know where money was going. Hoyle' had replied that money was being held back to pay bills that were anticipated for the coming season. Knox was far from happy with this answer and he and others argued that if it were the case then the accounts should still show that fact.

It seems to have been the case that financial irregularities had been uncovered in the Australian league. A secret bank account had been discovered containing around £300. Hoyle had claimed that it was to cover the ground rents and such like for the coming season. However, it is possible that this was a fund to be used to pay players to sign for the new league and for unnamed other purposes and that the League committee were being deliberately kept in the dark.

Hoyle, having seen the writing on the wall, resigned before he was pushed. At the same meeting no one had been prepared to propose that Giltinan continue as secretary for another year and Horrie Miller was elected in his place. Finally, Tom Phelan was elected in place of Victor Trumper onto the committee, and became treasurer. The founding fathers of the game in Australia, Giltinan, Trumper and Hoyle were forced out of office. Giltinan returned home to a *fait accompli*, he now had no job, no income and, after the tour to England, no money either. In fact, he was hugely in debt as a result of the tour. The New South Wales Rugby League had refused to guarantee any financial losses the tour might make. It was a rather ignoble end to the careers of the three men most responsible for getting professional rugby organised in Australia.

The new incumbents were quick to respond to the Northern Union – they needed a tour sooner rather than later if they were to get their finances in order and, more importantly, fight off the attacks made on them by rugby union in Sydney.

Meanwhile, in Great Britain, the Championship Final had just been played. Wigan defeated Oldham in front of 12,000 fans to complete a season which had seen them win three trophies. In the euphoria that followed, the Northern Union committee met on 11 May 1909. The minutes record the disturbing news from down under: "A letter from the New South Wales Rugby League was read to the meeting. The contents stated there had been some serious mismanagement of the league's affairs and that Messers Knox, Miller and Phelan had been elected vice president, honorary treasurer, and honorary secretary respectively. A suggestion was also thrown out that we try and complete arrangements for a visit to Australia next season. After consideration of the letter it was felt it would be best to write to the New South Wales League that with a view to their getting their affairs and league into a satisfactory and strong position it would perhaps be the wisest course to defer our visit still further."

When the Northern Union committee met again on 10 June they had received a further communication: "A letter was read from the New South Wales League giving particulars of their progress and expressing the hope that the Union would send a team over to Australia at the end of season 1909–10. The secretary was instructed to say that it would be unwise to make the visit in both their and our interests until the New South Wales League was established on a firm financial basis."

The tour was once more thrown into jeopardy, It seems that Baskerville had made it all look so easy with his All-Golds tour. It is perhaps a measure of just how great his organisational skills had been. The Northern Union seemed to be meeting untold difficulties in their attempts to organise a tour.

It has to be said the Northern Union had little idea of, and possibly little interest in, the events transpiring in Sydney. They did not realise just how important the tour was to the development of the game in Australia. As shall become clear, once it was known that the tour was definitely to take place, it allowed the developing Australian rugby league to recruit former rugby union stars into the game. They transferred their allegiance and in so doing brought over many thousands of fans to watch the new code.

There was one item which brought to light a number of issues within the game down under. Perhaps it also coloured the NU's opinion regarding the tour for a time. It was a letter James Giltinan sent to the Northern Union asking for their assistance. The request, considered by the committee at their meeting on 13 July 1910 was: "A letter was read from Mr J.J. Giltinan in which he pointed out he would lose to the tune of £385 in respect of the tour of the Australian team in England and he asked the committee if they could assist him in this matter. The committee instructed the secretary to say they regretted they were unable to do so."

The Northern Union, just as the New South Wales League had done, turned their back on Giltinan, a man who had done so much to launch the Northern Union game down under and worked so hard to

19

make the tour of England a success. His financial situation was in no small part due to him paying out of his own pocket to ensure the Australian tour could keep operating as long as it did. Sadly all the predictions the Australian newspapers had made prior to that tour about its precarious financial situation had come true. Now the Northern Union were about to turn against him in his hour of need. Then, as today, the Northern Union had the view that the game was a business. They showed a ruthless streak, and quite clearly had little sympathy with failure or financial impropriety. Their decision had serious repercussions as Giltinan was declared bankrupt in Sydney and never really recovered. The game in Australia lost a potentially great administrator and benefactor that it could ill afford to jettison.

As the 1909–10 season in England was looming events took a turn for the better. In September the New Zealand Rugby League had been formed and the Northern Union received a cablegram from them asking for affiliation. The committee decided to await the letter which was to follow before committing themselves to such action. The letter duly followed and spelled out the request in full: That the New Zealand Rugby League be formed affiliating with and adopting the rules of the Northern Rugby Union.

They asked that the league be recognised as the ruling body for the whole of New Zealand and that leagues forming in other centres throughout the dominion affiliate to them as the ruling body.

They also asked that "they themselves make all rules, bye-laws and regulations for the local conduct and welfare of the league business, always providing that no power whatsoever shall be implied or vested in their League to alter in any way the actual playing rules of the game unless with permission and in compliance with the rules of the Northern Union."

While the committee was generally in favour and sent a cable informing the new league as such, they could not agree to Auckland having control of the whole of New Zealand rugby league and said so. They said that: "...representation of such should be on a broad basis, giving each province [of New Zealand] an equitable representation..."

New Zealand now seemed to be organised on a basis which was acceptable to the Northern Union. In February the NU had received a letter that said: "We understand that your league is sending a team to Australia this coming season. We should very much like to have you extend the visit to New Zealand."

This meant that the Northern Union was now more favourable toward the idea of including New Zealand in their tour. They were, however, still somewhat reluctant to make a decision, less likely make a financial commitment, to such a venture. It was one thing to host a tour – the outlay was relatively small – organising a tour overseas was a huge financial commitment. The NU's indecision was causing a problem for both countries on the other side of the world. They needed a decision, and for a variety of reasons, they needed a tour from the Northern Union.

When the NU committee met on 12 October 1909, they were in receipt of two cables from Australia and New Zealand pressing them to send a team out on tour. The New Zealand cable offered the NU 60 per cent of all gross gate receipts for a six-match tour. They also were in receipt of letters from Giltinan and Harold Rowe expressing support for such a tour. Even in the middle of his deepening financial problems, Giltinan was still pushing the cause of the game down under. They had no need to make any decision at the meeting simply because of a further cable, this one from Alexander Knox of the New South Wales League, it simply read: "Do not do anything until you receive my letter."

When Knox's letter arrived, in November, it said that he was shortly to visit the country and would be pleased to discuss proposals for the tour in person. The Northern Union deputed Messrs Houghton, Cooke, Wood and Platt to meet Knox and report back to the full committee.

It must have been extremely difficult trying to conduct negotiations at that time either by cable or letter, the delay caused by such methods must have been frustrating to all parties. The uncertainty created by such delays was shown early in November when Joseph Platt who, speaking after the Yorkshire versus Lancashire County Championship match, said that he was not sure if the tour would take place – hardly a vote of confidence from the NU's secretary.

After Knox's visit, however, things seemed to move on at a greater pace. By the middle of December 1909 the New South Wales Rugby League became affiliated to the Northern Union and a sub-committee was created to deal specifically with the tour. Financial proposals were drafted, agreed to by the Northern Union, and posted to Australia and New Zealand respectively. The proposals were:

"The Northern Union to take: 65 per cent of gross gate and stand receipts if takings do not exceed £10,000; 60 per cent if takings over £10,000 but do not exceed £12,000; 55 per cent of takings if over

£12,000 but do not exceed £15,000 and 50 per cent of takings if over £15,000. All charges for ground and advertising and all other local expenses to be paid out of the percentage taken by the New South Wales and New Zealand Rugby League respectively.

These terms were certainly favourable to the Northern Union. Indeed, they would have felt they were taking the greater financial risk. Things seemed to have moved relatively swiftly and on 16 December 1909, the minutes of the meeting show how much expense was involved in sending a team to tour down under. The relevant minute read: "The secretary was instructed to get exact dates of sailing at the end of April, beginning of May next and the amount of time that could be saved going overland to Marseilles or Brindisi." The committee made an estimate of the cost of the trip as follows:

27 player steamship fare @ £80 each	£2,160
Fares in England	£45
Up country fares in Australia	£260
Fares to New Zealand	£368
Fares in New Zealand	£200
Outfits and washing	£200
Contingencies	£100
Hotel bills	£540
Payments to players	£1,325
Two managers (fares etc.)	£450
Total cost	**£5,648**

The secretary was instructed, based on these figures, to send a cable to New South Wales as follows: "Committee considering tour for next season, post suggested programme."

This was an enormous outlay for the Northern Union, so it is no wonder they were cautious about committing themselves to the tour, but committed they were. However, negotiations were still ongoing with the Leagues in Australia and New Zealand. When the NU committee met on 29 December 1909, a year and a day after the first official recorded mention of the tour, they had a counter-offer to consider, as the minutes show: "A letter was read from the New South Wales Rugby League giving estimates of receipts for the Australian and New Zealand tours as £8,100 and offering, after taking 15 per cent for ground charges, to allow 60 per cent of the balance. They put down the sum of £3,500 as our expenses."

It was decided to cable a reply: "Expenses would greatly exceed your estimate, terms inadequate."

This would not have been a surprise; even the Northern Union did not expect the Australians to simply agree to the terms sent to them. So while the arrangements for the tour continued to move on, the vexing question of finance was still unresolved. There is no doubt that all parties were playing games but the Northern Union felt it had the strongest hand. After all, the NU committee felt that Australia and New Zealand needed the tour much more than they did. They must have felt that they would eventually come round to the Union's way of thinking, hopefully sooner than later. So confident was the Union that in February they asked Lance Todd, the New Zealand centre playing for Wigan, to attend a committee meeting in Manchester.

Todd was questioned about his thoughts, ideas and knowledge of the state of the game in his native land because he was in regular contact with the game's players and officials in New Zealand. It is not clear if Todd managed to sway the committee in any way, or if it was a communication from Australia which did it. However, at that same meeting, it was finally confirmed that the tour was to go ahead. The minutes recorded: "A cable was received from the New South Wales Rugby League accepting the original terms offered by the Union in a letter of 18 December. It was decided to confirm same in writing and to cable New Zealand Rugby League offering six dates or less on the same terms."

So the Northern Union had got its way on the financial aspects of the tour. They had little doubt that the New Zealand response would also be in the affirmative. It is important to note here that six fixtures were offered to the New Zealand Rugby League.

During that same meeting there was also another tour item which read: "Mr Clifford appeared before the committee with respect to becoming one of the managers of proposed Australian tour and he promised to give the matter his careful consideration. Mr Houghton expressed his willingness to make the trip as one of the managers."

It is interesting that Joseph Houghton expressed a desire to make the trip as tour manager. Did he actually declare an interest when making his request to the committee? Mr Houghton had two excellent reasons for wishing to make the trip – his sons Thomas and Samuel. Both of them had emigrated to New Zealand and perhaps he saw this as a golden opportunity to visit them at the union's expense. Intriguingly, they had both originally signed for Houghton's St Helens

23

club. It could well be that they had been impressed enough by Baskerville to try their luck in New Zealand.

Thomas Herbert Houghton, the eldest son, was a threequarter who was now playing for Ponsonby in New Zealand. In 1909 he went on the New Zealand tour to Australia and, although no test matches were played on the tour, he did play for his adopted country against a New South Wales side. In 1908 he represented Auckland against Taranaki and was for a time the Auckland Rugby League delegate on the New Zealand Rugby League Council, resigning in 1913. It would seem that in addition to that he was also on the board of the North Sydney club in Australia. Just how he could be in two places at the same time and serve two masters is a mystery.

His brother Sam also played for Ponsonby and was the first treasurer of the Auckland Rugby League. At the time of the tour he was the treasurer of the New Zealand Rugby League. Both, it seems, were of great value in those early days following the death of Albert Baskerville. There is no newspaper reference to the father ever meeting up with his sons, but it seems likely that he did. Incidentally, Houghton and Clifford also led the second tour down under in 1914, which was cut short by the outbreak of the First World War.

So, on 15 February 1910, the final obstacle was removed and the tour could now be planned in earnest The Northern Union was going to send its players to the other side of the world. Many of the committee probably believed that at last they would be able to show rugby union that they had cemented a place in the British sporting scene, and now on the world scene as well.

There was a great deal to be done, passage had to be booked for the tour party and more importantly the tour party needed to be selected. All the clubs were asked to nominate players they thought suitable to undertake such a tour, players who "would do honour to the Northern Union both on and off the field, so that the Union would have the reputation of not only having shown the best football, but of having sent out the best-behaved and most gentlemanly team that has toured Australia." They were still conscious of the feelings toward them by the establishment in general and rugby union in particular. They now had the opportunity to show the world the qualities of Northern Union rugby and its players.

The tour committee met on the following day to set in motion such practicalities as booking passage to Australia. Equally important were the payments that would be made to the players, which had to be sufficient to warrant them leaving their employment for the four months or so they would be away. Equally, the payment must not be too much that it ate into the potential profits from the tour that might accrue to the Union. A delicate balance needed to be made.

The playing strip and boots needed to be ordered. It was decided that the playing jersey would be red and white hoops with the Northern Union international badge sewn onto it. All of these tasks were to be addressed and then recommendations brought before the full committee on 22 February, 1910.

At that meeting, Joseph Platt reported formal acceptance by the Australian and New Zealand Leagues of the terms of the tour that had been first proposed by the Union back in December. The minutes of the meeting also reveal the travel arrangements that were to be made for the tourists: "It was decided that the party be booked second salon passage on Orient Liner leaving London on the 15th April except in respect to players engaged in the Union and League finals, who would travel by the P&O, April 22nd or Orient Line April 29th, as circumstances may require. The sub-committee were instructed to send players overland to Marseilles where necessary."

The other important matter decided at that meeting were the terms which were to be offered to the players. The implication was that this was not negotiable, the offer would be made, players could take it or leave it. The terms were very carefully minuted to avoid any doubt:
"The terms to be allowed to players were fixed as follows:
The Union to pay all travelling expenses, reasonable hotel bills, provide football outfits and pay for all washing and laundry.
Players to have an allowance of 10 shillings per week on shipboard and £1 per week upon land, an additional allowance of £1 per week be paid to families at home in respect of players who are married.
One-third share of the profits of the tour (if any) to be divided amongst the players in such manner as the committee shall determine.

"Mr Houghton was appointed one of the managers of the tour on the terms that all reasonable expenses of the journey be met, and a sum of fifty pounds allowed as provision for his family whilst away.

"It was decided that the team be left with the sub-committee, that each player be interviewed by the committee and advised with respect to kit required. It was decided that the team number 26 players.

"The uniform agreed upon was fixed to be red and white hooped jerseys, black pants and black stockings with red band.

"It was decided that a couple of special matches be played, one at Headingley Leeds and the other at Wigan, between the two teams going out, or a team selected from the colonials at present in England.

"It was suggested that the County Unions and the Northern Rugby League would doubtless be prepared to advance as loan any surplus funds they may have toward meeting the initial expenses of the tour."

So there was progress made on the details of the tour, all that was needed now was to select the players. The tour party would be selected by the sub-committee rather than playing trial matches, or at least that is the implication from the minutes. This proved to be the case, players being selected by committee even before the trial matches had been played. The players were to be paid something like £4 for the eight weeks they were on board ship and £8 for the eight weeks they were in Australia and New Zealand along with a percentage of the tour profits, if any. They would also get another £16 given to their family while they were away, but only for the married players. That came to around £28 per married player, yet the managers would receive "all reasonable expenses" along with a further £50 while they were away. Maybe the cost of living was greater for a committee member in 1910 than it was for a player, although they would have some extra expenses, such as entertaining officials from the other teams. All the key decisions had now been taken.

The newspapers were having a great time speculating about who would be selected for the tour. 'Forward' writing in the *Athletic News* in March 1910 considered the possible make-up of the party, but also said: "The question of a return being made via America is now under consideration, for an editor of a well-known American paper is anxious to arrange a series of exhibition games." Just what would the game be like today if the Northern Union had decided to go to America and succeeded in establishing it there?

A week later the sub-committee began to complete the arrangements. The minutes show the orders placed for the playing equipment:
"The following orders in respect of outfits were given out.
26 pairs of boots to Mansfield @ 9/6d per pair
6 dozen jerseys @ 60/- per dozen
3 dozen stockings @ 25/- per dozen
26 pairs of shoulder pads @ 2/- per dozen
26 pairs of drawers @ 7/6d per dozen
3 dozen pants @ 65/- per dozen"

Just three days later, on 3 March, the sub-committee met again, this time in Manchester, and interviewed the first of the players they had decided to take on tour. The minutes recorded that Jim Sharrock and Johnny Thomas from Wigan, Bert Avery from Oldham and James Lomas from Salford were all interviewed and accepted positions in the team. They also selected a group of players who could be added to the party after being interviewed, but did not release their details. Those players were Billy Batten (Hunslet), Chick Jenkins (Ebbw Vale), George Tyson (Oldham), Tommy Newbould (Wakefield), Fred Webster (Leeds), Billy Jukes (Hunslet), R. Padbury (Runcorn), Frank Shugars (Warrington) and James Davies (Huddersfield).

The committee also confirmed the travel arrangements for the tourists. They booked on the Orient liner, Osterley, leaving London on 15 April. One manager would leave with the bulk of the party and the other manager to travel overland to Marseilles with the other players, those who were in the Challenge Cup and Championship finals, joining the Osterley there. In fact, the second party were unable to meet the Osterley and had to sail on the SS Malwa from Marseilles. They also agreed for the first trial match to be at Headingley on 14 March.

At the same meeting they interviewed a reporter by the name of Marsh, who worked for *Athletic News Weekly*. He offered to write a tour souvenir brochure for the Union which would be published by *Athletic News*. The committee must have been impressed by his presentation as they looked favourably on his proposals and asked him to get back to them with the terms for the publication.

The committee met again on 7 March. The main business was to interview more prospective members of the tour party. It was minuted that: "Tyson, Oldham, R. Padbury, Runcorn, Joe Ferguson, Oldham, F. Shugars, Warrington were interviewed by the committee in respect of the Australasian tour. Tyson, owing to business reasons, was unable to accept the invitation. Ferguson could not give a definite decision, Shugars accepted the invitation and in the case of Padbury he informed the committee he had been suffering from blood poisoning and it was consequently decided to withdraw the invitation in his case for the time being." The other tour business was to select two teams and reserves to play in the first trial match at Leeds on 14 April, between a First Selected side and Yorkshire Probables.

The full committee, the following day, decided that they would have a special meeting in The Dog and Partridge, in Wigan on 21 March, after the second trial match where they agreed terms with

Athletic News to produce the tour brochure. The brochures would cost the NU £4 per 1,000 for the first 20,000 with any additional copies costing £3 per 1,000. The reporter was also given the go-ahead to write the material that would appear into the brochure.

A week later Tommy Newbould and Chick Jenkins appeared before the committee and also accepted the invitation to tour. It seems that the selection process for this first tour was torturous to say the least, if not for the players, certainly for the committee members. Not all players, it seems, were totally enamoured with the prospect of touring the colonies. On 18 March, 11 days after making the invitation to Joe Ferguson, the committee had still not heard from him. They decided at that time to withdraw the invitation and look for a replacement.

By the time the committee met on 22 March, the tour party was more or less complete. The minutes recorded: "It was decided to invite the following to accept places in the team for the Colonial tour: F. Young (Leeds), F. Farrar (Hunslet), Joe Riley (Halifax), F. Smith, (Hunslet), E. Curzon (Salford), F. Boylen (Hull), H. Kershaw (Wakefield), R. Ramsdale (Wigan), W. Winstanley (Leigh), T. Hulme (Oldham), G. Ruddick (Broughton Rangers).

It was decided that Messrs Cooke and Wood would interview the Yorkshire players at Leeds on Thursday and Messrs Houghton and Platt the Lancashire players at Manchester on the same day."

By the end of March the final player, Huddersfield's John Bartholomew, was invited to tour, and accepted. However, it was only now, when players really considered what they were getting into that some realised that being away would cause hardship for their family left behind. The committee agreed to grant Dick Ramsdale, the Wigan forward, an extra 10 shillings per week "toward support of his father and mother whilst away on tour". They did the same for a number of other players who also pleaded a case of hardship for their families.

The final task of the sub-committee, so they thought, was to arrange a suitable send off for the first ever Northern Union tourists. After much discussion it was resolved to call a special general meeting of the full committee to consider this and other matters for the following Tuesday. At that meeting on 5 April the send off was finalised. Dinners were organised for the team members in Lancashire and Yorkshire, and the team headquarters in London was to be the Imperial Hotel in Russell Square. The Challenge Cup Final date was arranged for 16 April to allow a strong team to be sent out for the early matches.

In the final, Leeds were to play Hull, but the two teams fought out a 7–7 draw. This necessitated a replay but as the Championship Final was being played on the following Saturday, the NU decided that the Cup Final must be replayed just two days later on Monday 18 April. The replay saw Leeds emerge victorious 26–12. One party of tourists had left London, but those players involved with the two finals had to leave later, and arrangements had to be made for them.

There was however an added problem for the committee. In the tour trial that had been played at Leeds, on 14 March, the winger Billy Batten had injured his knee. The injury had cleared up sufficiently for him to play for England in the international against Wales in Ebbw Vale on 9 April. Sadly in that match Batten broke down again. Two days later, on 11 April, he informed the committee that he would not be fit to tour.

The following day the committee met and discussed the medical report which they had received on Batten's knee from Dr Littlewood of Leeds. They concluded they had no option but to withdraw the invitation to tour, but luckily decided to leave until a later date the task of selecting a replacement. It was just a few days later that the committee recorded in the minutes a twist in the tale. Batten had attended the Challenge Cup replay and informed members of the committee that he was fit enough to tour and asked to be reinstated. On 18 April, he appeared before the committee and the minutes recorded: "W. Batten again approached the sub-committee with respect to going out to Australia, saying his knee was now fit and that he would be fit to play. He offered to play for Hemsworth verses Normanton St Jude's to test it."

The committee agreed to this and asked Mr Shaw and Mr Nicholl to watch him play and report. It was agreed that if the report be favourable he would be examined again by Dr Littlewood.

The following week when the committee met again they considered the medical report on Batten and interviewed him again. Given that he had scored a hat-trick of tries and kicked a couple of goals in the trial match and the doctor was happy enough with his fitness, he was reinstated, and told to leave for London with the rest of the party just two days later. So, finally, at the last minute, everything had come together and both groups of tourists were on their way to Australia.

In 1910 Australia was still the Commonwealth of Australia. Australians still considered themselves to be closely tied to the United Kingdom. At that time most Australians had at least one British grandparent. They were very much part of the British Empire and used the same national anthem. The tourists found travel was somewhat different to home. While the East Coast had reasonably well developed rail links, people still tended to move up and down the coast by sea rather than on the railway, possibly because it was cheaper to do so.

When the tourists arrived in Sydney, they would have found a thriving city of around half million people with many buildings similar in style to those back home. The streets, however, were broader and straighter, creating a patchwork effect across Sydney. The place was a hive of industry with shipping and the wool trade prominent. Building work, particularly in the suburbs, was very pronounced.

The docks worked day and night to cope with the freight and passenger trade. Transport was by electric tram and cable car although horse and cart – known as a drag – was still common. They would have found little to be different from Leeds or Manchester apart from the beaches and, of course, the temperature.

Brisbane was similar, although on a slightly smaller scale with a population of around 200,000. Ship and boat-building was one of the main industries along with the wool and tanning industries. The tourists could have been forgiven for assuming that all Australia consisted of thriving cities and communities much like home.

However, once out of the cities they would have quickly witnessed a different scene, as much of Australia was still bush interspersed with areas of cleared land for farming or sheep and cattle-grazing. This was not much changed from when Captain Cook visited in 1770.

The train lines were pushing ever deeper into the interior of the country as well as along the coast, but were not widely used for passengers, rather for transporting goods and animals. There was a great contrast between urban and rural Australia.

When the tourists arrived they found they were greeted with a great deal of affection because they were British. Also, there was the feeling that Northern Union rugby allowed the Australian game to develop in a way which suited Australians rather than having the RFU in London impose its will upon them. The RFU may have wanted to assist the Australians, but was under pressure from both the Scottish and Irish Rugby Unions about professionalism.

While the language and culture they met was British, the tourists found the heat and the country's vastness something new. It was to be an eventful tour.

3. Life on the ocean waves

As the Championship Final came to a close and Oldham went home with the spoils, the players selected to tour from Oldham and runners-up Wigan met to form the second party to sail to Australia. They were joined by Billy Batten who had managed to prove his fitness. One of this group, James Leytham of Wigan, kept a diary, which provides a unique insight into parts of that journey and the journey around Australia and New Zealand.

Leytham loved the sea and was about to embark on the greatest journey of his life. It is ironic that he would eventually die in a boating accident. In August 1916 he and seven of his family went out fishing at the Lune Estuary close to his home town of Lancaster early on a Sunday morning. As the tide began to change and the party were about to head for home catastrophe stuck. His boat The Pearl was swamped by a wave and capsized. Leytham was a strong swimmer but refused to leave the group who were clinging to the upturned boat and sent another man to swim to shore. He perished along with six members of his family.

Leytham was not labelled 'Gentleman Jim' for nothing; he was a very modest man and this is reflected in his diary. There is little reference to the exploits of the team on the field, it is more a record of what he did and saw on the tour, mainly off the pitch. It must be remembered that Leytham, like his colleagues, was an ordinary working man who happened to be a very good rugby player. Few of the tourists, if any, had ever been outside Britain, let alone to the other side of the world. They were about to see places and countries they had never experienced before.

Leytham wrote: "Left Lancaster 10.30 on Wednesday 27th April. Arrived Wigan, had lunch and boarded the train... at 2.10. There was a large crowd of friends... We left Manchester at 4.15 and a crowd... sang *They are Jolly Good Fellows*. Arrived London at 8 o' clock... we had a ride to the theatre and got back to our hotel at 11.30... We had all our tobacco, matches and cigarettes to take out of our trunks. We got all the rules from the Cooks man. We were not allowed to take more than 1½ ounces of twist, 20 cigarettes, 19 cigars and no matches."

He continued: "We left London 9.00 on 28th... arrived Dover at 10.45 then boarded the steamer for Calais, when half-way across Jenkins and Sharrock had to go down and part with their breakfast.

Arrived Calais at 1.o'clock where we had to go through the custom office but we were passed through. Boarded the train... for Paris at 6 o' clock... a three-course dinner cost us 5/- each then boarded the train for Marseilles."

Some of the frustrations that the rugby union players must have felt at this time are shown here. They were allowed only three shillings a day expenses. On this trip a meal cost five shillings. It was one way of controlling the game the rugby union authorities were reluctant to give up. By keeping the allowance so low it effectively precluded working class men from pursuing the highest honours in the game because they simply could not afford to go on tour.

Leytham went on: "We had 14-hour ride and... arrived Marseilles at 9 o' clock on April 29th. We were driven through the town to the docks and boarded the S.S. Malwa... It was very calm and we travelled 17 miles up to 12 o' clock..."

During the tour some players were commissioned to write articles for their local paper. One was the Oldham forward Bert Avery. In a letter he wrote to the *Oldham Chronicle* while in Port Said and published on 11 May 1910, he says pretty much the same as Leytham. He did, however, also say that they were not bothering with training for a week or more, but that the players were: "taking salt baths so as to soften our muscles, before we get to Australia. We shall get ourselves fit so as if called on to play the day or so after we arrive we shall be ready."

Joseph Platt had accompanied the players on their trip to France. It was reported at the time that as the Malwa was leaving port and Platt was standing on the dockside waving off the last of the tourists that a tug assisting the ship began to list badly and eventually sank. The event seemed to have taken some of the shine off a story that English rugby players were leaving France for Australia.

Leytham's love of the sea showed as he recorded the distance travelled by the ship each day. At the end of his diary there is a daily log of the sea miles travelled each day on the outward journey to Australia. He described the ship's progress: "On April 30th... our watches began to lose time. We were up at 7 o' clock, after breakfast we went up on deck and started larking, playing rings and cricket then it started getting very warm and up to 12 o'clock we had travelled another 371 miles. We got into the Straits of Messina and passed Italy and Sicily at 1 o' clock on Sunday morning, it was a great sight and got to bed at 3 o' clock.

A group of the tourists on board ship. (Courtesy Oldham RL Heritage Trust)

Wigan's players on the tour: From top left: Bert Jenkins, James Leytham,
Jim Sharrock, Dick Ramsdale and Johnny Thomas in the centre

Next day, Sunday May 1 was a bit windy, after breakfast... the bell began to ring for church. It was a very nice service and was over in half an hour, we had travelled another 368 miles. The rest of the day was quiet. I went to church at night... After church went on deck and about 10 o'clock we saw the first boat. It was well lit up, it was one of the P+O steamers.

Next morning May 2 about 7 o' clock we passed an island and saw another steamer about 10 miles away and then went down for breakfast. Then had a meeting with all the second class passengers to arrange sports. In the afternoon we had a game of cricket, it was windy and the water was rough...

May 3, a very fine morning and warm. We were playing games up to 12 o' clock and then we... landed at Port Said at 1.45. We got off our boat and got a guide to take us round the town.... All the cab men were fighting which had to take us, so we all got out of them and the police came up and stopped the row. So we walked a bit more and then got three more cabs and then our guide got into more trouble. I thought they were going to choke him... I thought they were going to go for us but the police came up again... All the married women wear a cane down their nose they have all their face covered up except their nose and eyes and they look rather queer."

In 1910 travel to foreign parts was fraught with danger for the unwary. He was fascinated by Egypt: "One place was the church where the Egyptians and Arabs pray. They put us some shoes on and we went through and up to the top of the tower. Our guide went with the priest and washed his hands, feet and mouth and then went to pray whilst we went round the town. I will never forget it as long as I live, we don't know we are alive. So we drove through the streets and it looked very risky (They call the church Mohammadan Mosque) the place looked very dirty, they buy the bread in the street and were covered in flies...

Well we got back again and paid our guide 4/- and told him to meet us tonight. So we got on board and said we would not risk it again. We had dinner at 7 o' clock and [were] talking things over. So I went up on deck and met a Rev. that had just come aboard. He was going to Australia and I told him ours doings in Port Said. He said we were very lucky, he said they do a lot of killing people. I was glad to land but gladder to get back on board."

It would appear that Leytham had learned the lessons from his stop at Port Said and that discretion was the better part of valour: "May

34

4th: Very hot we could not sleep... We had a few more passengers then we set off again leaving Port Said at 10.15. We had not gone very far down the Suez Canal before I saw a porpoise spinning round... I have never been in as hot weather. All the way down the Suez which is 89 miles long and [at] not... more than 6 miles an hour, it was a grand sight. There is a railway from one end to the other, there are only trees where the stations are and all the rest is desert... We left Suez Canal about 2 o'clock in the morning.

May 5: We are now in the Red Sea and have lost sight of land. The sun is very hot... We have started with our sports, there is all kind of games two of our men have got into the final for the Bull Ball and coide.

May 6 and 7: Very hot we started training on the 6th but had to give it up on account of the heat. We... watch[ed] a lot of flying fish on the 7th. We saw a few steamers and twelve large lumps of rocks which they call the 12 apostles."

The players had a week off from training, but clearly chose the wrong time to start up again because they were forced to give up the struggle against the heat in the Red Sea. But at least they were at sea, much cooler than on land.

"May 8: I heard of the King's [Edward VII] death at 3.30 in the morning I was sleeping on the deck which we are doing every night. We arrived Aden at 10 o' clock, we stayed there about three hours to unload the mails and to tranship passengers... There was church at night... A Scottish parson preached and a blind man played the Dead March... there was a wireless telegraph on board and that is how we got to know about the King.

May 9: ...It is very hot and we are hoping for cooler weather, we are now in the Arabian Sea. We could see the African coast. We had our photo taken with our football clothes on... about 5 or 6 men [took them.] We got the copy from one of them [who] was a doctor and are going to print them ourselves...

We arrived at Colombo on May 14 at 8 o' clock in the morning, we had breakfast and then went ashore where a reporter met us. He told us he was with the rest of the team on May 4 and he said Mr Houghton told him to look after us and he took us round Ceylon to buy cigarettes. We got them cheaper on land than we could get them on board. Then we all hired a rickshaw and an Arab [took] us all round the town. We saw all kinds of fruit growing in the roadway. Coconuts in plenty we could buy pineapple for 2d each..."

Leytham was fascinated by what he saw and experienced once the ship docked. He was keen to get out onto land and explore the sights: "I hadn't been there long before one of our chaps came up in his rickshaw and paid him 2/8d both the Arabs wanted a tip after paying them. We met another passenger off our boat, a Scotsman [who] was staying in Ceylon and he took us to his hotel and had lunch... it was 85 degrees in the shade... we got a cab and drove round and it was a great sight... we drove on to see a rugby match with some Englishmen and then came on a heavy shower of rain so we ran for shelter. After the match we went back to his hotel... we just got back for 7 o' clock dinner."

This entry shows just how strong the influence of rugby union was. The public school boys who learned the game then went to university and after graduation travelled to all parts of the Empire. Wherever they went they took the game with them, even to the remoter parts such as Ceylon (now Sri Lanka). Baskerville's team, when they stopped off in Ceylon in 1907, actually played a XV-a-side union game against a team in that country. That game was played on 12 September 1907 at Colombo. The tourists defeated Ceylon 33–8. As a result the Ceylon team were banned by the Rugby Union for professionalism once it became common knowledge. However, it did not stop them continuing to play the game; after all they were thousands of miles from London.

This gives an insight into Leytham and what interested him. He was prepared to get up at 3.30am to experience Halley's Comet streaking across the night sky. The next time it would appear would be in 1985.

Leytham's next entry continued: "... we left Colombo on 14 May Midnight and are on the longest stretch 9 days to Fremantle without seeing land. We are now in the Indian Ocean. We see many a grand sight, watching the sun set.

On Sunday 15 May it was windy and rough... Next day May 16 turned out calm and hot. Went alright till 21 May then we started rolling about, there was a lot sick. So we arrived at Fremantle on May 24... It still kept raining, the people told us they have had it for two weeks. So we set sail about 5 o'clock the same day with about 300 more passengers, a lot of them going to the gold fields and also a lot of children. As soon as we got out we started rolling about, nearly all the passengers were laid up with sea sickness.

Clearly Fremantle did not really please him, not the best introduction to Australia. At this time there was no direct rail link between Adelaide and Sydney, the only way to get to either place was to go by sea or rail to Melbourne and then to either Adelaide or Sydney from there. The rail link between Perth and Adelaide was not completed until the First World War.

Leytham described their travels round Australia: "We had two days rough and two days just fair, we arrived at Adelaide on May 28 at 9 o' clock... It is a very fine place there is plenty of land to cultivate. It is a dear place. We started on our journey at 6 o'clock the same day. There [were] two of the British battleships just lying out of the docks. We arrived in Melbourne 30 May at 7.30. We went right to the dockside and then we went ashore... it is a fine place. We went to the theatre at night and got back to the boat at 12 o'clock at night.

We went all round Melbourne in the afternoon, round by the park and all the principle old buildings. We left... on May 31 at 12 noon..."

After the initial disappointment of Fremantle the country had a profound effect on him. He would have loved the cities of Adelaide, Melbourne and Sydney because he was near the sea. When the ship sailed from Melbourne Joseph Houghton was not on board. It had been arranged that he would travel overland by train to Sydney. This meant that he would travel more quickly and be able to finalise the arrangements for the tourists once they arrived.

Leytham described their arrival in Sydney: "We arrived at Sydney on 2 June at 7.30. Our manager came to meet us and took us to our hotel, Grand Hotel Waverley, Sydney, about three miles out. All the boys [from the first party] were in good condition, they have been training twice a day. We had dinner and then off we went to the theatre where we saw Tommy Burns and Bob Fitzsimmons and they are to. At night we were invited to a smoking concert by the South Sydney RFC." [The rugby league club rather than the rugby union club which also existed at the time.]

So it was that a journey that had begun in Lancaster on 27 April ended on 2 June when the tourists settled in to what would be their headquarters for the next few weeks.

The Grand Hotel today. (Photo: Tom Mather)

4.   Let the games commence

When the players on the Osterley docked in Sydney on 26 May, just a few days ahead of Leytham and the remainder of the party, they were greeted by a large crowd at the dockside. Once ashore, John Clifford and Joseph Houghton, who had travelled over land from Melbourne to finalise arrangements in Sydney, were there to greet them. They, along with the players and all their equipment were loaded into drags – horse-drawn vehicles – and travelled along George Street and on through Sydney to their headquarters for their stay. They also carried with them a wooden box in which was securely fastened a silver cup that was to be presented to the New Zealand Rugby League on the second leg of the tour.

The tour party made the Grand Hotel, at the corner of Bronte Road and Ebley Street at what is now Bondi Junction, their home while in Sydney. The hotel is still there today and now hosts an Irish pub on the ground floor. As they settled in, the two managers had a number of problems before the tour had really started. The major one was that while 20 players had sailed in the first group they were now down to 19. The Oldham forward Tom Helm, the only Scot in the party, had injured a knee in a match prior to leaving England. It seemed that he had aggravated the injury on board ship, probably during a tug-of-war contest involving the passengers.

The second problem was that both managers had no idea where the remaining six players were. They were due to arrive on 2 June, but Clifford and Houghton had no way of knowing if they would. Also, Billy Batten was in that second group, but they were unsure if he would be fit enough for the rigours of rugby in Australia. It was one thing to play in an amateur match to test a knee, quite another to play at the highest level on the hard grounds in Sydney.

The third problem was that, unlike today, when the tour captain is often announced before the rest of the tour players have been selected, no captain had been named for this first tour. That decision had been left to Clifford and Houghton. They decided to adopt the club system used at the time and sounded out the players over who they thought should captain the party. The consensus was that the best man for the job was James Lomas, the Salford centre who already captained his club. So Lomas was chosen as captain for the tour.

Having arrived on the Wednesday, the following day after their first night's sleep on dry land for more than six weeks, the tourists were taken into the centre of Sydney to be officially welcomed to Australia at a function held in their honour at the Arcadia Hotel. The tourists entered a packed hotel to a rapturous reception.

The reception welcomed the tourists, but the ongoing issue of professionalism in rugby in both New South Wales and Queensland raised its head. The English managers could have been forgiven for thinking they had been transported back to the early 1890s in the north of England and the breakaway from the English Rugby Union. The reception was reported in the *Sydney Morning Herald* of Friday 27 May which related that James Joynton Smith, the NSWRL president, officially welcomed the tourists to his country.

In doing so he immediately launched into an attack on rugby union, echoing to a large extent the belief in the Northern Union that the differences between the two codes were wide. Joyton Smith said: "The present tour marked an epoch in football, and the public would see a game played such as they had never seen before."

It was a tall order for the players of both countries to live up to. However, it must be remembered that the battle between the two codes in Sydney was by no means over – the bitterness between the two still raged. That bitterness was also to some extend fuelled by the newspapers, some siding with one code, others with the rival game. Rugby union had, in an attempt to thwart the new game, organised a tour of NSW not only by a New Zealand Maori squad but also by a party from American universities.

Once Joynton Smith sat down, the political element was brought to the fore by the Labor Federal Attorney General Billy Hughes. He also entered into the professionalism debate in his speech of welcome, saying: "I must confess to leaning always toward the professional. I want the men who do play to do so very well and there is no reason why they should not be paid."

He went on to talk about 'quacks' who would endorse the situation still prevalent in English cricket whereby professional cricketers and amateurs entered the field of play by different gates. Hughes also said: "I do not believe in advocating a sport which is only for those who can give their services for nothing." This was a far cry from the response Wray Palliser had made to Albert Baskerville's tour party to Great Britain in 1907.

It was then the turn of Fred Flowers to rise to his feet. Flowers was a Labor Member of Parliament who had become a patron of the newly formed League. He also had little to say about the touring team, but launched into an attack on the way the newspapers had treated the new Northern Union game, its players and officials

With the Australian part of the reception over it was the turn of the Englishmen to respond and Joseph Houghton did so. He too spoke of the ongoing professionalism debate in Australia, saying: "The league is only paying over the table what others were doing under the table. It is better to take it openly than have it put in shoe or sock."

It was left to John Clifford to speak about what the tourists had come to do, which was play rugby. He told the assembled crowd: "We have brought a team which will be a credit to the old country, when they know in England what a great reception we have had they will say there is a strong branch [of Northern Union rugby] out here."

The reception over, the players then returned to Waverley where they were staying. At the Waverley Oval they were again formally welcomed, this time to the suburb of Waverley by the mayor, Alderman Watkins.

What was clear to the tourists was that it was not simply playing the game which would prove important in Sydney; they would also help the Northern Union code overcome rugby union as well.

Then it was down to the serious business of training, something which had, to a large part, been seriously neglected. This was a deliberate ploy by the tourists who felt that they had a long tour ahead of them and needed to peak at the right time if they were to win the test series. It was a ploy which almost backfired in a big way.

The New South Wales Rugby League had entered into an arrangement with a reporter called Frank Bickford, who worked for the *Sydney Telegraph,* to cover all of the matches played on tour. He produced much of the material that players such as Bert Avery sent home along with their own letters to the local papers in the north of England. The major problem was that this news was sent back to England by ship, so it was always five or six weeks out of date. However, Avery's letters to the *Oldham Chronicle* are excellent insomuch as they put an English slant on proceedings, particularly on the field of play, something Leytham did not. This counteracts the Australian view of events which was reflected in their newspapers.

On their first Saturday in Sydney, the South Sydney club hosted the tourists and gave them a welcome. They were the club's guests at their match against Newtown. At the after-match function that Joseph Houghton said: "The Northern Union regard this [the tour] as a missionary tour and is prepared to lose £1,000 over it."

41

He went on to say that the tour had not been organised on the cheap but, on the contrary, the party was, in his view, the most powerful team that the Northern Union could produce. The English newspapers supported this view.

The tour had already had one success insomuch that once it became known that it was definitely going to take place it saw a good number of Australian rugby union players switch codes. So strong was the league game that the new code no longer felt it necessary to go out and 'buy' rugby union players. It was strong enough to tell union players that they could join rugby league – or not – but it was no longer prepared to pay them a signing-on fee as they had in the past.

How well the league game was doing is shown by the events that occurred on Saturday 28 May, just two days after the arrival of the first contingent of Northern Union tourists. On that afternoon New South Wales and Queensland met in a rugby union match, the first representative game of the season. The game attracted 10,000 spectators. The Newtown club game, by contrast, attracted 17,000 spectators; the league was winning the battle for the public's hard-earned cash. Equally important was the fact that they were now winning over the once-hostile Sydney press. More often than not, articles tended to support league action and condemn union.

In the week leading up to the first game Houghton and Clifford arranged to have a meeting with the NSW referees society to try to iron out any differing interpretations of the laws. Sadly Clifford had had an accident and was unable to attend so it was left to Houghton to put forward the NU's view. It seems incredulous that, given the Australians were in only their third season of NU rugby as opposed to the 15 years in England the game had been played they would need to iron out differences. But then, as now, they did.

During the meeting Houghton seemed to have sorted out any difficulties, bar one. That was the issue of what happened when players were injured during a game. In Australia the rule was that injured players could be replaced, so they had a practice of naming their teams along with one 'emergency' forward and back. Houghton would not agree to this and insisted that the tourists would abide by the rules of the Northern Union. So throughout the whole tour the hosts could and would replace injured players, while the tourists would play with men short if there was a serious injury.

Just two days after the full complement of players arrived in Sydney the first game of the tour was scheduled to kick-off. As

Saturday dawned the newspapers were full of coverage of the greatly anticipated first clash under Northern Union rules on Australian soil between an Australian team and the British. As the day progressed the anticipation grew to fever pitch as more and more spectators began to make their way, many on foot, towards the Paddington area of the city, passing the Victoria Barracks and on to Moore Park. Others travelled out of the city while others came in from the suburbs. At the north end of Moore Park was the Royal Agricultural Showground, affectionately know to the locals as 'The Agra', which was the venue for the match between New South Wales and the Northern Union.

There had been big matches there before. In 1907 the All-Golds had played the Australians there before moving onto England. The New Zealanders had toured, as did a Maori team two years later, but this was different. Now the organisation responsible for the new rugby code in Australia was to take the field.

One aspect of the struggle between rugby union and the newly formed rugby league in Australia had been that the union authorities had further alienated the public by their open attempts to deny the new league grounds on which to play their code. Often they would lease a ground with no intention of using it for playing themselves, simply to deny it to the newly formed league. By 1910 there were still skirmishes between the two codes, but league seemed to be coming out on top. The crowds were flocking to watch their code while rugby union were struggling to keep their star players.

The arrival of the Northern Union and the tour was the opportunity for the NU code to be established as the leading football code. The anticipated profits from the venture would go a long way to securing the future of the league and its finances. It would allow it to grow and expand the game along the country's eastern seaboard. As 3 o' clock approached on 4 June the agricultural ground was beginning to fill. The cash was dropping into the turnstile boxes in a seemingly increasing stream. There was a curtain-raiser before the main event when two teams made up of "the next best 26 New South Wales players", formed two teams. That game over, the crowd settled down for the main event. The tourists did not select any of the latecomers who had left England after the Championship Final. The teams were:

New South Wales: Neill, Messenger, Hickey, Broomham, Russell, W. Farnsworth, McKivat, Cann, Barnett, Courtney, Spence, Noble, Sullivan.
Northern Union: Young, Bartholomew, Lomas, Chic Jenkins, Farrar, Thomas, Smith, Webster, Ramsdale, Jukes, Winstanley, Boylen, Ruddick.
Referee: Tom McMahon.

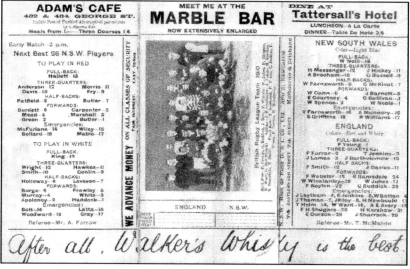

The programme from the New South Wales versus England
match on 4 June 1910.
(Courtesy Don Hammond, NZRL Museum)

The Northern Union team that played New South Wales on 4 June.
(Courtesy Graham Morris)

The New South Wales team were first to take the field looking resplendent in their navy blue shorts and light blue jerseys, with the Kangaroo boldly emblazoned on their chest. They were led onto the field by their mascot, a live kangaroo. The Northern Union were greeted by a tremendous roar as the crowd got their first glimpse of the team, their red and white hooped jerseys contrasting sharply with the colours of their opponents. They were led onto the field by a man dressed as a lion and the band playing *Three cheers for the red, white and blue*.

This opening encounter, the first of three meetings between the two sides went as expected. The tourists were to some extent still finding their land legs, having only had 10 days ashore, while the home team really were motivated for the match. The spectators were struck by the sheer size of some of the players and not just the forwards. NU skipper James Lomas looked every inch a colossus.

There was a strong southerly wind blowing which Lomas made good use of, having won the toss. As he kicked off, according to the *Sydney Morning Herald* there were 37,000 supporters packed into the ground. It quickly became apparent that the meeting Houghton had had with the referees had been a complete waste of time. The tourists struggled to get to grips with the way referee McMahon interpreted the scrum and scrimmage rules.

In the match report the *Sydney Morning Herald* wrote: "While admitting that the referee was above reproach in fairly dealing with the match, there were a few cases in which his decisions did not meet with the approval of the visitors. This was particularly noticeable in the putting the ball into the scrum. On many occasions on Saturday the ball was thrown against the leg of a forward and bounced back and at once a pass rush was started. This misunderstanding made a big difference to the visitors. The ball should have been recalled, the scrum reformed and the ball put in so that it would not come out until it had passed the first line of forwards. Why there should be a difference of opinion on a point of this importance is hard to understand. The visitors will show out better when they understand the interpretation placed here upon the rules."

That said, the tourists did start the match strongly and, with the wind at their back, forced the New South Wales team to concede two early penalties. Lomas converted both to give the visitors a 4–0 lead. That was as good as it got for the Northern Union. The lighter, fitter and faster Australians soon began to dominate the game and exposed the tourists' lack of fitness. Dally Messenger and Chris McKivat were causing problems and the latter fed Russell, the wingman, a pass which saw him race in for the first try of the game.

Not long after Russell was again involved and his charge led to half the New South Wales team handling the ball before Courtney crossed for a try. The visitors were struggling to come to terms with the referee, the hard ground, smaller ball and the speed of the opposition. Half-time arrived with the score at 8–6.

The second half went much the same way as the first, the only thing favouring the tourists was that the strong wind dropped as the sides changed ends. As the game wore on, the home team's superior fitness showed through and they won 28–14. The 14 points flattered the tourists, five of them came from a try which resulted from a pass that was "as far forward as from here to Oldham" according to Bert Avery in his letter home.

The tourists had not helped themselves by sticking rigidly to the no-substitute rule for injured players. Late in the first half their winger Fred Farrar injured his shoulder and did not appear for the second half, forcing the tourists to play with 12 men for 40 minutes. The man who replaced Farrar on the wing, Billy Winstanley, the Leigh forward, was himself limping from an injury and more or less a passenger.

Then, in the second half, the NU's full-back, Frank Young, was injured and taken off for treatment leaving just 11 men on the pitch. The *Herald's* reporter noted: "This was a blessing in disguise, just where he [Young] was standing behind the goal line. Messenger was about to finish a brilliant effort with a try, when Young with much presence of mind, rushed forward and forced the New South Wales captain back into the playing area."

Given that the tourists played half the game with 12 men and, at one stage had only 11, with one of those limping, it was a creditable performance against a strong side whose players had been playing for the last six weeks or so at club level.

In all probability everyone went away happy. The New South Wales team had a victory and the tourists were happy with their first outing. The spectators had witnessed a home win which will have pleased them, as did the quality of the rugby played. More importantly, the NU managers were delighted at the gate receipts of £1,383. Suddenly all was looking rosy for the tour. There was just one problem, the reporters had picked up on the visitors' lack of fitness and made their views clear.

Leytham wrote about that first match. He said that all the players were at the ground by 1pm. He estimated that around 50,000 spectators were present. This estimate was based on the newspaper reports of the game, which exaggerated the crowd. The Agricultural Showground could not hold that number of spectators. The crowd would have been higher had the league been able to use the Sydney Cricket Ground on the other side of Moore Park.

Bert Avery, who sat out this first encounter, wrote a letter to the *Oldham Chronicle* just after the match. His letter gives an account of the play and an honest assessment of the tourists' performance. He wrote: "It is no use beating about the bush, our lads were not in condition, for another thing, the Colonials seemed to be a lot faster and they are more used to the hard grounds."

The decision to hold back on training was already causing problems for the tourists. Avery was also critical of the referee. He was voicing concerns that were to remain with the tourists all through the trip. He said of the referee for the first match: "...and the referee not being quite up to the rules he was letting the half-backs put the ball in just as they wanted.

New South Wales versus England 6 June 1910

England near the line (Photo: *Sydney Mail*)

England about to tackle (Photo: *Sydney Mail*)

Chris McKivat on the attack (Photo: *Sydney Mail*)

English defenders surround Russell
(Photo: *Sydney Mail*)

Sometimes the ball never went into the scrimmage at all and at times it went clean through and he let it go on... Russell got tackled in possession and threw the ball away. Courtney came up and walked over the line with the ball, whilst everybody stood looking at him expecting the whistle to blow, but the referee allowed the try much to the disappointment of the crowd..."

Still the result was a win for New South Wales and a rude awakening for the tourists.

There was another shock awaiting them just two days later when the two sides met once more, again at the Agra. The match had been arranged because the Monday was a holiday and another bumper crowd was expected to attend. Not surprisingly the Australians did not change their line up. The tourists, wanting to give as many players as possible a game, made changes to their team. It read:

Bartholomew, Batten, Lomas, Bert Jenkins, Leytham, Thomas, Smith, Webster, Ramsdale, Jukes, Ward, Shugars, Ruddick.

The result was the same: a defeat for the tourists, this time 27–20, in front of an estimated crowd of 40,000, slightly bigger than that on the Saturday.

While the local press waxed lyrical about the Australians' performance, they held nothing back about that of the visitors. The *Herald* on 6 June said of the home side: "Never did a NSW side, whether at [the] league or union game, show such consistent brilliance. It reminded one of the magnificent dashes of some of the New Zealand teams we have had in Sydney. Perfect conditions, confidence, quickness of action yet with coolness, were seen after the first 15 minutes. The longer the game went the greater would be the victory."

The reporter was not so enthusiastic about the visitors' performances in both encounters. He felt: "On reputation the visitors played much below their form. It was too bad to be true."

Things got even worse following the defeat on the Monday. The press was even less enthusiastic of the talent sent over by the NU. The *Sydney Mail's* reporter, writing on 8 June said: "To date the Englishmen have not shown the form that was expected of them, no one anticipated that top form would be shown until the tour was advanced two or three weeks. On Saturday however, they were out of the hunt when the game had been running 15 minutes... The Englishmen came with the reputation of being the cream of English football. On Saturday their cream had gone sour, for they were beaten handsomely..."

Frank Bickford of the *Sydney Daily Telegraph* did not agree with many of his countrymen about the tourists' performance in the second match. In his account published in the *Oldham Chronicle* on 23 July, he said: "It was the opinion today here of the majority of the audience that the better team lost... Before going any further I must mention that the ball used here is somewhat different from the one used in the old country, which made a material difference in the kicking of the Northern Union players, but it is one which will be quickly overcome... The old country team sadly felt the loss of Young who was incapacitated in Saturday's match..."

While the situation was not out of control, the first two games had seen the visitors soundly beaten 28–14 on the Saturday and 27–20 on the Monday. They had not shown anything like the form expected of them. Also, if the NU team did not improve quickly, would people still turn up in large numbers to watch them? Clifford and Houghton must have been worried about the effect this would have on the tour profits.

One thing was for certain, the players were under no illusion what was expected of them and took the newspapers' criticism of them to heart. Avery said: "I can assure you we got it hot from the papers about our poor form... We made up our minds it was work with a capital W during the week for the third match."

As the tour was getting underway not all of the fixtures had been finalised. The Northern Union was not sure who they were going to play, and where. It was a far cry from the picture that 'Forward' had painted back home in early April when he wrote in *Athletic News*: "The Australian sub-committee have so far advanced their arrangements that only minor details connected with the tour now need attention."

The Sydney press, as has been seen, were beginning to ask questions of the visitors and suggesting if this was the best the NU had to offer then it was pretty poor fare. *The Referee* in its columns expressed the view that the Australian public could only hope that the tourists would begin to show just why folks back home in the North of England considered this group of players to be 'The cream of Northern Union Football'.

When New South Wales and the tourists took to the field on 11 June the Northern Union side knew what was at stake and knuckled down to the task with a vengeance. It became obvious to the 27,000 spectators that the hard work done since the last defeat had honed the visitors. It also quickly became apparent they had come to terms with the hard grounds and the smaller ball.

The Australian ball was not just smaller than the tourists were used to it was also less round. The English ball was not really that far removed from an association football. It was less rounded and shaped more like a pudding, the Australian ball was more like the modern ball in use today. The tourists had also got to grips with the referees' interpretation of the rules. They simply swept aside the opposition, with precision passing and ferocious tackling and recorded their first win of the tour. It was the strength of running by both forwards and backs that NSW could not handle. At last the tourists were playing up to their true form and making their superior weight tell.

The Sydney press were in no doubt about the man-of-the-match: the skipper Jim Lomas. He turned in an outstanding performance in leading his side to a 23–10 win. The press once again talked of him being a colossus, as did Bert Avery in a letter in the *Oldham Chronicle* on 23 July: "We were much improved and for over threequarters of the game we were complete masters of the situation. Our captain was playing a fine game, he was here there and everywhere and always where required... The event of the day was Lomas, securing on his own 25, with characteristic dash made for the line. Man after man tried to down him and I should say at least half-a-dozen actually grabbed him, but he brushed them aside and sailed over. This solo effort fairly roused the crowd who cheered themselves hoarse and it deserved it."

The reporters were as enthusiastic after the match as they had been critical before it. The only worry had been the size of the crowd, which was smaller than expected, but hopefully all would now be well and the public interest had been recaptured. Houghton and Clifford must have sat back and preened themselves over their choice of captain, and breathed a sign of relief that the coffers would continue to be filled at a pleasant rate. Lomas was less happy about the situation. He was a modest man and the attention he was attracting did not sit well with him. In an attempt to avoid the attention his popularity was generating he would shave off his moustache to hide his identity.

According to the attendance figures reported in the newspapers around 100,000 people had watched the first three games. However, there were still some problems for the tour managers. Avery wrote:

"We have had quite a chapter of accidents with Davies and Helm getting hurt at practice on the ship, and since we started playing on land Farrar, Bartholomew, Chic Jenkins, Ramsdale and Bert Jenkins have been injured and not available for the third game.

It is the hard dropping that knocks you at times but we now have a good trainer and are finding Turkish baths a nice and soothing cure for sore and bruised bodies after the game."

The visitors did not get through any of the first three games with a full compliment of players. More often than not they had lost one player for a long period of the game and in some cases two. Given the circumstances they had performed creditably after six weeks at sea. However, the Australian press had not seen it that way.

It was not all training and playing for the tourists in the days leading up to the crucial third game. Leytham in his diary described visiting an asylum called Gladeswell. They later went to the Theatre Royal to watch a performance of *The Third Degree*. When the play finished they returned to their hotel by boat down the Parramatta River. And one day, after training, the tourists went on a boat tour around the harbour and stopped off for dinner at Corry's Gardens. Leytham reckoned it was the best meal they had eaten since they left England. Bert Avery felt the same way, as did the other players – high praise indeed. He also reckoned all the players were looking forward to the third match against New South Wales.

Now the players were beginning to enjoy themselves on the field as well as off it. The NSWRL was absolutely delighted with the size of the crowds at the Agricultural Ground and the ground's board was also delighted with their percentage of the gate receipts. It was a measure of the effect the Northern Union brand of rugby was having on the Australian paying public. On the same Saturday the NU tourists were recording their first win at the adjacent Sydney Cricket Ground, the Australia versus New Zealand rugby union test attracted just 17,000 supporters. In 1907 the corresponding fixture had drawn a crowd of 52,000. The decline in union's fortunes as a result of the rise of Northern Union prompted one rugby union official to be quoted in the Sydney papers saying: "We'll keep going, even if we are forced to play to empty houses."

It was a quote that was to come back to haunt rugby union as the NU tour was coming to a close in Australia. The clash with the other code was never far from the tourists' minds as Avery and others wrote back home: "We fully expected, when we arrived that the rugby union out here would do all it could to 'kill' our trip, financially at all events all our expectations have been realised but theirs have been sadly misplaced."

For now, however, everything in the garden was rosy, but it would not last. Trouble was brewing on the horizon. The next fixture on the tour seemed innocuous enough. The opponents were the grandly titled Metropolis, a team made up of players from the clubs in the Sydney Metropolitan area. It turned out to be a battle royal.

It is important to understand the hard-line approach the authorities in Australia had towards violence in any form, in everyday life or on a rugby field. This attitude tended to be supported unreservedly by the newspapers who saw it as their duty to support the governing authorities. One way they tended to do this was to refrain from publicising acts of violence on the rugby field.

The reasons for this are unclear, even after all this time, but there are some clues from both newspaper reports of events and also of the draconian punishments handed down to players in the union code dismissed for fighting. It appears the rugby authorities were under pressure from the government to ensure order on the field to make sure spectators, inspired by acts on the field, had no reason to infringe the laws of the land.

Supporters down under, like their counterparts in Lancashire and Yorkshire, were quick to vent their feelings at any perceived injustice on the field or with referee's decisions they disagreed with. At the time there had been a number of occasions when rioting had nearly occurred at football matches and the authorities took a very dim view of this. The seriousness can be gauged from a Press Association report from Melbourne on 3 June 1910, albeit referring to an Australian Rules game in Victoria. It read:

Putting Down Rowdyism
The chairman of the Victorian Football League, in disqualifying a player for two years for striking another player, said: 'If players want to be fighters let them be fighters, but if they want to be footballers let them play football.'

As the outcome of a consultation between the Premier and the head of the police, concerted measures will be taken to put down rowdyism, either by players or spectators, firmly."

Just over a week later another Press Association report from Melbourne carried a similar theme: "The latest football case is that of the umpire of the rowdy match who was fined £2 for striking a spectator. The umpire was fighting his way out of a hostile crowd, when he struck the prosecutor."

Both the government and sports bodies were not prepared to have any kind of civil unrest. If that unrest was generated by a football match then it would be severely dealt with, because the football match would have attracted a sizeable crowd. To some extent the approach engendered in Victoria was also taken up in New South Wales. Both the government and the NSW Rugby League were less than happy with any sort of play which they felt might reflect badly on the fledgling code and also upset good order in any way.

This is probably one of the reasons why the newspapers of the day were a little reluctant to go into much, if any, detail regarding rough play or players being dismissed. That way they could not have an accusation of creating civil unrest levelled against them. That being the case the manner in which they reported the fourth game of the tour gives an indication of just how bad the foul play really was. After all this time it is impossible to say, with any certainty, just why such violent play occurred in this match.

The match against the Metropolis was scheduled for Wednesday 15 June. The following Saturday, just three days later, was to see the first test match between the two countries in Australia. Maybe the Metropolis players saw the opportunity to soften up the NU players. Or maybe the NU players wanted to assert their authority after the defeats in the first two games. Whatever the reason, when the referee blew his whistle to start the second half, both sides lost interest in the ball and laid into each other – fists and boots flew with monotonous regularity. The first half appeared to have been the lull before the storm.

Leytham, who was not playing in the game, wrote in his diary: "...it was a very rough game, two of our men got hurt, Bartholomew and Young, and [we] played the second half with 11 men. There was plenty of fighting and kicking. The police were talking of stopping the game, but England won."

At the time this match was talked about as being the dirtiest in the – albeit short – history of Northern Union rugby. Fights broke out all over the field, punches and kicks were liberally administered by both sides and the police talked of stopping the match. This was witnessed by around 3,000 supporters, but what did the thousands of league followers read of the match in the press? The report the following day,

16 June, in the *Sydney Morning Herald* was, on the whole, very low key. The report read:

International Football

England v Metropolis

The English league team played the fourth match of their tour at the Agricultural Ground yesterday afternoon with a strong team representing the Metropolis as their opponents. There was an attendance of about 3,000. England won by 34 points to 25.

The play was generally very fast and at times very rough.

All through the second half the game, as described elsewhere, was exceptionally rough, and the Englishmen were deservedly hooted by the crowd. Boylen for the visitors and Hickey, one of the local players, were ordered off the field shortly before the end of the game for fighting.

The teams for the big match were as follows:-

England: F. Young, W. Batten, Bert Jenkins, Chic Jenkins, J. Bartholomew, J. Thomas, T. Newbould, A.E. Avery, F. Boylen, H. Kershaw, E. Curzon, F. Webster, G. Ruddick

Metropolis: H. Hallet, F. Munnary, J. Hickey, H. Messenger, A. Wright, W. Farnsworth, Holloway, A. Burge, P. McCue, R. Williams, J. Barnett, S. Griffiths, R. Craig.

The report said that the tourists started well: "Newbould took the ball on the run, and passed to Batten. Bert Jenkins took it from the latter, and, dodging smartly, got over the line. Thomas added the extra points. In a second attack Thomas snapped the ball from the ground, and was over. The kick for goal went astray." Metropolis then scored through Holloway, with Messenger adding the goal. The tourists then attacked and scored again: "Thomas taking the ball from Bartholomew, put in a splendid run down the line. He ended up by scoring almost in front of goal, but Bartholomew, who took the kick, failed to increase the score, which was now England 11 points, Metropolis 5."

Then Young was injured, he "... had to be carried off the field. He tried to side-step, and wrenched his knee badly. Bartholomew took his place temporarily at full-back, but Young shortly came back on again." Despite being a player down, the tourist scored again through Avery, although the conversion was missed. Then "play was again interrupted through an accident to Bartholomew."

Young's injury seems to have been accidental – he twisted a knee in open play. After having treatment he tried to return and after a short time could not carry on. Later newspaper reports said that he had damaged an already torn knee cartilage. The injury effectively ended Young's tour as his knee did not recover sufficiently for him to play again until it was almost over.

On first examination after the game the doctor felt that the injury was so bad that he would be unable to play again on tour. Young was forced to spend a week or so laid up in bed and only allowed up after that on crutches. He spent 10 days or more using crutches and struggled to be really fit for the rest of the tour.

On the other hand the injury to Bartholomew is not so easy to explain. While some reports say he was injured fairly in general play, it could be that the players did not see it that way. He was injured while attempting to stop a forward rush and was either kicked or kneed in the ribs. Whichever it was, it was done with sufficient force to break three ribs. His injuries meant that he returned home with only five appearances to his credit.

Again the home side put pressure on the tourists: "Wright, who finished a pretty series of passes, in which five of the local men handled the ball, scored in front of goal after a fine run of about 25 yards along the wing. Messenger converted. Still the attacks went on. Holloway sent the ball to Farnsworth, who in turn passed to Hickey and he scrambled over between the posts. Messenger was again successful with the kick. The game became faster and harder, and in a few minutes England were minus two men, Young having been carried off again with an injured knee. They remained on the aggressive, however, and Thomas sprinted across the field, passed to Webster, who got over in the corner. Batten this time took the kick, and scored the extra points." At half-time the tourists were 21–15 ahead.

Curzon scored, to extend the tourists' lead. Then: "Messenger was given a free kick well forward. Instead of kicking for goal he took the Englishmen by surprise by punting over the line, and, following on fast, scored easily. He again added the extra points. This made the score 24–20 to the tourists.

The reporter was now forced to mention the rough play: "The game was becoming rougher all the time, and fists were frequently used. For obstruction, Metropolis were awarded a free, and Messenger put up a fine goal. Messenger punted down the field, and, as he followed on, was tackled by Kershaw. Both fell, but Kershaw, rising to his feet quickly, attacked Messenger with fists and feet Holloway, however, had got over the line whilst the fight was going on. Messenger kicked for goal but missed."

Webster and Newbould added further tries to give the tourists a comfortable winning margin of 34–25.

Given all that had supposedly gone on the reporter's coverage is a master of understatement. The *Sydney Sportsman* reported on the game on 22 June, a week later, when the dust had settled somewhat and calmer minds were able to review the scene, was much more forthright in its appraisal of the game and who was responsible for the mayhem. The *Sydney Sportsman* was a weekly publication that came out on a Wednesday. They ran the story under the following headlines:

"Wednesday's Wild Work"
"The Referee Shirks His Duty"
"A Britisher 'Puts the Boot In'"
"From Football to Fisticuffs"

This report is much more factual and says the trouble was not widespread, but confined to the forwards. One of the Australian players who was sent off, Hickey, is quoted summing up the trouble thus: "I'll tell yer what the trouble was lads, the referee got confused."

The reporter was critical of the infamous second half: "Immediately the second half had commenced the dirt began to creep in. Sundry swings and uppercuts were handed out in the most generous fashion, and referee Farrar, instead of making an example of one of them by a trip to the pavilion, gazed calmly on, and waited for the game to continue. Certainly now and then he did look angry at a couple of scrappers, and even went so far as to tell them to be good boys and not smack one another, but it was only after Kershaw had nearly kicked the stuffing out of Messenger, and every man in the team had had a kick or crack that he caught Hickey and Boylen hitting out of their turn, and bunged them off." This was typical of the way rough house play was reported in 1910.

Sean Fagan, the Australian rugby historian, wrote about this match in his book about Dally Messenger. He also made the point that the press at the time were reluctant to mention rough play, or players being dismissed from the field – if the press wrote about it, it must have been bad, he noted. Messenger himself later said of the game: "It was hailed as the dirtiest game in history." But even Dally was unable to say just how or why the game seemed to erupt.

According to Messenger, the first half went off without any problems, although how that could have been is a little difficult to understand. From Leytham's account the tourists had lost two of their backs, Bartholomew and Young, in the first half so were up against it defensively. Perhaps the constant need to defend their line against superior numbers caused frustration and this boiled over into violence There is also a good deal of evidence to suggest that the referee was out of his depth and unable to exercise any control. In the second half fights were breaking out between players after almost every tackle and the referee, instead of setting an example by sending players off, simply did not act.

Messenger, recalling events much later, believed that the real trouble started when the tourists' forward, Harry Kershaw, seemed to totally lose his temper. He had been sent out onto the wing to replace the injured Bartholomew. Messenger had put a kick down field and Kershaw misjudged the flight – as he was gathering in the kick he got Messenger at the same time.

As both players fell to the ground Kershaw ended up on top and proceeded to drop the ball and punch Messenger in the face. He then rose to his feet and started kicking Messenger in the legs.

This account of events is supported by reports in the *Herald* on 16 June: "Messenger punted down the field, and, as he followed on, was tackled by Kershaw. Both fell, but Kershaw, rising to his feet quickly, attacked Messenger with fists and feet."

Messenger was the idol of the Australian supporters, even then he had almost mythical qualities in their eyes. To many Australian supporters he was responsible for the success of the professional game there. Now they could see their idol being punched and repeatedly kicked while on the ground. They rose up almost as one and roared their disapproval. At one point it was feared that the crowd would rush onto the field and extract their own revenge on Kershaw.

This was exactly the scenario that the police authorities were firmly clamping down on. It was probably the reason the police were on the point of stepping in and stopping the game. Who knows what would have happened had they done so?

When the dust settled, the referee called Kershaw over and the crowd fully expected to see him sent off. Possibly because the tourists only had 11 men on the field, or because he lacked the courage, he simply administering a caution. The crowd went absolutely wild and whenever a NU player or, in particular, Kershaw got the ball the crowd hurled insults and abuse. Messenger said much later that he felt Kershaw was a little concussed from a knock earlier in the game, and it was that which could have led to his assault. There is no doubt that it was an angry mob of supporters – fortunately it was a relatively small crowd. If a 40,000 strong crowd had witnessed the scene, what might have happened?

One spectator at the game was under no illusion as to who were the perpetrators of the crimes. He wrote in reply to an earlier letter and his response was published in the *Herald* dated 21 June: "Your correspondent who signs himself HH states that the Sydney crowd are notorious all the world over for their unsportsmanlike behaviour. I wonder how many crowds would stand the spectacle of one man down being booted mercilessly, and later on the sight of Hickey being attacked by only three of the Englishmen. It would make any crowd hostile..." He, like many other Australians, was under no illusion that it was the tourists who were to blame for the debacle against the Metropolis. Many union supporters took the opportunity to write letters to the papers complaining about the thuggery they had witnessed, and it was a difficult time for the league game. However, the reporters, perhaps being more clear-headed and less fanatical in their support of one team or one code, laid the blame at the referee's door.

What is evident from the match is that neither the tourists nor the hosts were going to back down from a confrontation. The complete reasons behind the violence in this game will probably never be clear. The tourists faced a torrid 40 minutes in the second half with only 11 men, so perhaps may have felt they needed to even up the numbers if they were to have any chance of winning. It could have been the case that when the tourists went into the dressing room at half-time and seeing the extent of the injuries to Young and Bartholomew were intent on exacting retribution, feeling they were getting no protection from the referee.

On the other hand, maybe Metropolis, seeing the depleted team in front of them and being unable to break down their defence lost their heads. This led to punches being swung and kicks being aimed at players rather than the ball in frustration at being unable to cross the tourists' line. Whatever the causes, the game, and its memories remained with the players throughout the rest of the tour and beyond.

In his diary, Leytham revealed some interesting facts, not least that the police were on the point of stepping in and stopping the match. Had they done so, there is no doubt that players would have been charged with criminal offences and brought before the magistrate. What would have happened to the tour then is anyone's guess. One thing is certain, the authorities were not going to simply sit back and do nothing, not with the first test looming on the near horizon. Then there would be a massive crowd and the potential for trouble much greater. The police must have feared that a partisan 40,000 plus crowd, perceiving any injustice by the touring team may well take matters into their own hands. There would not be enough police to stop them. The police did not sit back. They approached both the Northern Union and New South Wales Rugby League managements. There is no doubt that what was said, alongside a warning from John Clifford, had a profound effect on one of the teams.

The aftermath of the game and the fall out from it would continue in the days leading up to the all-important first test. The repercussions were such that even when the tourists returned to Leeds, Houghton felt compelled to speak of it when giving his end-of-tour dinner speech

There were two other outcomes in the aftermath of the Metropolis match. One was close to home, the other more than 1,000 miles away in New Zealand. One place initially unaffected by events was in the heartland of the Northern Union. The NU committee had overlooked the need to send a recognised newspaper journalist out with the tour party. Had they done so, then at least they would have obtained a steady stream of information and reports on the tour more quickly than they eventually appeared in the British press. The reports would have been sent by wire and published on the next day or so. To be fair Frank Bickford of the Sydney-based *Telegraph* did an excellent job and his reports were evenly balanced. As it was, people in England complained at the limited coverage the tour was receiving in the press.

The reason for the lack of coverage in England could well have been that the cost of sending a wire report was prohibitive. When the Australians toured England and Wales in 1908, the public in Australia received very little first-hand coverage of the matches.

Houghton and Clifford in Sydney were probably wishing the coverage stayed minimal of the Metropolis match, but another issue was brewing in Auckland. As the tour was progressing in Australia so anticipation was growing in both the North and South Islands in New Zealand. Each week that passed was a week closer to the tourists arriving on their shores.

However, both the police and rugby authorities were taking a similar line on violence and foul play as their counterparts in New

South Wales. In the run up to the tourists' visit to New Zealand there had been a spate of foul play in rugby union which in turn had led to some swinging suspensions. The culmination of this was the suspension of a player called Marshall. As a game ended and the players were walking off he attacked an opponent. He was arrested by the police and a charge of assault laid against him. When he appeared before the magistrate he was found guilty and fined £2. The New Zealand RU banned him for two years. Bans of such length were commonplace as far as foul play or abusive language toward the referee was concerned.

The feelings of the rugby league leadership can be imagined when on the Thursday following the Metropolis match the *Evening Post* in Auckland carried the following Press Association report of the Metropolis game. The report gave details of the match, then continued:

Riotous Scene
A Hostile Demonstration
The closing stages of the League match were of a riotous character.
Before the trouble reached its height, an Englishman, Bartholomew, met with an accident, two ribs being broken. Kershaw, who replaced him, in the heat of the play, struck Messenger in the face.

The failure of the umpire to order Kershaw off caused a hostile demonstration by the crowd and several encounters occurred.

Eventually an Englishman and an Australian were ordered off. The final whistle put an end to a disgraceful melee."

The Press Association seemed to be more willing to criticise players and the play when sending reports over the water. The antics at the Agricultural Ground must have been greeted with despair by the New Zealand League leadership and glee by their rugby union counterparts. The other thing which is apparent is the almost God-like status which was applied by the press to Dally Messenger. At times it seemed as if he was the only player on the field. Kershaw could not have picked a worse target to attack.

5. The Colonists are fair game

The tourists needed to prepare for the test match which was three days ahead. In Sydney the press sought to take advantage of whatever events they could. After all, there was a test match to build up to in three days' time on the Saturday. Many papers singled out Kershaw for special treatment; after all it was he who had clashed with Messenger. One newspaper said his actions were despicable and suggested that he should be sent home immediately.

One of the papers managed to track Kershaw down and get an interview with him. Unfortunately research has been unable to unearth the newspaper that carried the article and just what was said. Sadly, it is alleged, Kershaw was a little less than circumspect with his words. He boasted of his attack on Messenger and, when printed, the effect was like waving a red rag to a bull. The tour managers must have been furious with their man, certainly they took action themselves.

Given that a great deal was printed about the game and the aftermath there should be no reason why this interview should not be available in some archive, unless of course it never happened. Given that both Houghton and Clifford would not want to be seen to be bowing to external pressure, certainly not by the Northern Union Committee back home, perhaps they put out the story of Kershaw being indiscrete to give themselves an excuse to drop Kershaw.

They could then deny that they had been pressurised into changing the team by any outside authority, or even have to admit publicly that the police feared that Kershaw's appearance on the field might inflame the crowd. That is one possibility but it must be said, on balance, there is more evidence supporting that the interview did take place than it did not. Given the number of papers in Sydney at the time, and that the interview could have been published in the sports pages, or in the general body of the paper as a news story, it could well take months of searching to still fail to find it.

What is clear is that Kershaw had been pencilled in to play in the test match on the Saturday. He was promptly dropped from the team, probably for his indiscretion. And it is likely that he was dropped on police advice following his interview. The reporter for the *Sydney Sportsman* writing after the game said: "Kershaw was very wisely dropped out of the English team, and, from his candid admission to a reporter in an interview during last week, he ought to be dropped for the rest of the trip. A man who boasts of booting a fallen player is no footballer, and no good to the game here."

But on yet another front, the game's leaders and the police were less than happy with events. They were looking at a potentially nightmare scenario at the Agricultural Ground on Saturday afternoon. It was predicted that there would be a 40,000 plus gate for the test match. Should there be any similar action on the field as had been seen against Metropolis then the police would not be able to handle such a crowd. The fear was that they could rush the field.

Although the accounts mentioned earlier from Victoria that refer to Aussie Rules Football are true, it may well be a little too simple to apply the attitude of police and the authorities in Victoria to the same bodies in Sydney. The police did take action prior to and during the first test match and this did have a bearing on the outcome. Certainly the threat was a real one as far as the police were concerned and they were determined to take a proactive approach to the situation. Leytham in his diary outlines the perception in the tourists' camp: "...we expected a rough time – according to the papers it looked like as if we were going to be killed. They are going to have a large number of police... to keep the crowd off us. We had a letter sent us stating that if there was any striking or kicking the police [were] going to take action. Both sides were told about it..."

However, Clifford and Houghton had further problems to occupy them, as if they had not already got enough on their plate. While the test match was to be played in Sydney, arrangements had been made for those players not selected for the test to travel to Newcastle. The idea was that this second string team would play a game against Newcastle and District on the same day.

The problem was that the tourists did not have enough fit players to put out a second team. Young and Bartholomew were injured following the Metropolis game. The Oldham forward Tom Helm had still not recovered from his knee injury. So Clifford and Houghton solved the problem by arranging with the New South Wales Rugby League for guest players to turn out for the Northern Union.

When that second team took the field it included Australians Jim Devereux, Dan Frawley, Andy Morton, Alby Burge and New Zealander T. Byrne. Devereux and Morton had played in the threequarter line for Hull so they were no strangers to each other or the rest of the team. Neither was Frawley who played for Warrington. While it seems the tourists were stretching their resources very thinly they still were too good for the Newcastle side, running out winners 24–8.

Back in Sydney, as the day of the test match arrived, it was a little cloudy and overcast. Rain had fallen during the night, but a brisk northerly wind was blowing and it would dry out the ground and conditions would be perfect for rugby. As the players prepared for the game the crowd began threading its way through the city hours before kick-off. They came from all directions. They travelled on foot, walking up Oxford Street through Paddington before descending on the park. They came, as did the tourists, from Waverley and Bondi, all with one destination in mind.

They came by drag and alighted at the entrance to the park making the rest of their way on foot. They came, much to the delight of the league officials, in their thousands, all depositing their sixpences and shillings into the league's cash boxes. By 1pm the tourists were on their way, their drag making slow progress through the multitude thronging the streets to the ground.

It was only when the fans were gathered inside the Agra that they saw what action the police had taken. The *Sydney Sportsman* reporting the test match on the following Wednesday, 22 June, was appalled by what happened and ran both a cartoon and ditty, alongside a paragraph expressing their feelings about the proceedings. They wrote under the banner headline:

Bobbies on a new beat

The position appalling to players

"Rough play resulted during the rugby league match on the Agricultural Ground Last Wednesday. As a result, on Saturday last, the ground was surrounded by a small army of police. The police have finally decided on a campaign against any 'rough football'. They are empowered to arrest offenders, or summons them, and the section under which they may be prosecuted provides for a fine of £5 or 12 months imprisonment."

If this report is to be believed, the players clearly understood what the police action would be if they transgressed. And it had an effect on the players in the test match. Certainly it supported Leytham's claim about a letter being received by the NU managers. It seems that both teams were told that if they broke the law they would be arrested – the rugby field was to be no hiding place for them. The police considered kicking and fighting as being unlawful and would therefore act.

The cartoon about the police presence in the first test.
(From *The Sydney Sportsman*, June 1910)

In the ditty under the cartoon the reporter makes his feeling quite clear. He wrote:

Behold the trembling toeball blokes
With half a hundred cops around,
Afraid to run or tackle hard
Upon the verdant football ground.
The copper is the umpire now,
And should a man spill on his lug,
The man who spilled him swift will be
Grabbed by a John and thrown in 'jug'

66

Our umpire now will count for nought
But they will stand and tremble too,
'Rough Play' will be deemed by
Boss Sherwood's man – the 'boy in blue.'
So mind your eye, toeballers all,
Play 'lady-like', or for a cert
You will be fined or thrown in quod
Should in the game a man be hurt.

A hundred pleece now watch you close,
should you bump hard, it is their aim
To swift swoop down: so do take care,
And play a gentle girlie game.
And whilst the public watch you play,
And Johns on you their vigil keep,
Around the suburbs minus Johns,
The burglars will rich harvests reap

Prior to the test match kick-off there was a goalkicking competition between James Lomas and Dally Messenger. Lomas won 3–2. Writing in the 1930s about his time in Australia he recalled: "I beat Messenger for the championship of the world 3–2. It has never been played for since so I must still be champion. I got a silver cup and a gold medal."

What happened in the test match is best left to the reporter of the day. The following report appeared on 20 June in the *Sydney Morning Herald:*

International Football First Test
England Defeats Australia by 27 to 20.
"A match overflowing with thrilling and exciting incidents was the general verdict of the crowd of 39,000 as they made their exit from the Agricultural Society's Ground on Saturday. This great crowd, which by the way, included his Excellency, the Admiral, Sir Richard Poore, had been viewing the first test in the Southern Hemisphere between England and Australia under Northern Union rules.

Still the people, whilst admitting that it was a great match, and that the Englishmen had given an excellent display, were not carried away with the enthusiasm which marked the opening game of the tour, for they felt that the Australians had not played up to their best form. The spectators were moved by contending opinions – satisfied that the

67

winning team are a great side, and disappointed with the showing of the home team. "If there had been only another 10 minutes!" That was the thought at the finish. Then as on the previous Saturday, the home team were brilliant, but they left their run too late; they were unable to wipe off the points scored against them in the earlier part of the contest.

England won 27–20. It might have been a couple of points less margin of defeat had Messenger been more mindful of his last kick for goal than securing the ball, after the kick, as a trophy of what will be an historical event – the first test match under these rules.

The Australians who wore the combined colours of New South Wales and Queensland – light blue and maroon – had the wind in their favour in the first half and, at half-time they led 12–11. On changing over the Northern Unionists added 16 to the Australians' 8.

It was a great game, worthy of two international teams and it was won by the side that was fittest for the fray. The first match saw the home team in the better condition for so strenuous a game, while the visitors admittedly, were far from their best owing to the little while they had been off a long sea trip. Now they appeared to be in the pink of fitness, while, on the other hand, the home players showing suggests possible staleness. The Englishmen, or, to speak correctly the Anglo-Welshmen, won because they were better conditioned, and simply because they were the better side. They seized their opportunities. They made fewer mistakes than the Australians. Every time the visitors secured possession of the ball and started their passing rushes, even in their own half, there came a cry from the crowd, 'They're in', and the feeling was more pronounced when Lomas had the ball. Australia made some serious mistakes – mistakes of judgement and skill. The visitors upon gaining possession when defending cleared their lines of impending danger with a long punt into the enemy's camp. Not always so the Australians. Their punts were frequently weak when within their own half, affording opportunities for the simplest marks imaginable. Especially was this so with regard to Russell who at the 11th hour was substituted for Neill who was injured in the immediately preceding match at full-back.

The last line of Australian defence was the weakest point. In attack the passing rushes of the home team raised the hopes of the crowd only to be dashed to pieces by a failure to accept a transfer, which would have meant a try. It must, however, be admitted that the defence of the Englishmen on these occasions was superb. Nothing finer could have been seen than in the last 10 minutes or so. The forwards of the visiting team carried more weight than the Australians, and the visiting threequarters especially the centres, outpaced and outmanoeuvred the home backs. Perhaps the much talked of rough play of Wednesday caused the home team to be too mild in their tackling. There was a big difference between the two sides.

Lomas was the best man on the ground, and was splendidly supported by the other threequarters, Thomas, Batten and Leytham. The English captain is a man of many parts, of many dodges, and of great strength. With legs of great development, and with it speed, and a head for doing the right thing at the right moment, he took a power of stopping and of pulling down, while his tackling was more of the wrestle, for the man tackled invariably had to go down.

The visiting forwards were possessed of a greater weight than the home lot, and this told its tale. Jukes was the foremost: he was like a racing threequarter; and all the others were good. In scrum work there was not much to choose between the two sides. If anything honours were slightly in favour of the home pack. McKivat was smart, and in Farnsworth had an excellent ally in opening up the way for an Australian dash. Messenger was good, but not the man he was in the first match. Broomham showed fine form throughout and Woodhead, Queensland's sole representative, showed pace and cleverness in scoring a try. Hickey was solid without the brilliance of some of his former games.

Sharrock the English full-back, met with a severe accident during the first half, and was carried to touch, where he received the attention of the Ambulance Brigade. He admitted it was all an accident. During the interval he essayed to walk to the Sutter Pavilion, where the players had their quarters, but collapsed, and had to be removed on a stretcher. The incident cast a gloom over the crowd. During the second half his return, which was quite unexpected, to fill his place on the field was the signal for whole-hearted ringing cheers from the crowd.

The play

An appreciable northerly breeze prevailed when the players came out. The ground was fairly dry, seeing that rain fell the previous evening. *Australia:* C. Russell (South Sydney), C. Woodhead (Queensland), J. Hickey (Glebe), H. Messenger (Eastern Suburbs), A. Broomham (North Sydney), W. Farnsworth (Newtown), C. McKivat (Glebe), J.T. Barnett (Newtown),

W. Spence (South Sydney), E. Courtney (North Sydney), C. Sullivan (North Sydney), R.R. Craig (Balmain)

Northern Union: J. Sharrock, W. Batten, J. Lomas, B. Jenkins, J. Leytham, J. Thomas, T.H. Newbould, F. Webster, W. Ward , E. Curzon, R. Ramsdale, W. Jukes, A.E. Avery.

Referee: T. McMahon

Touch judges: Mr Bolton and Mr Seabrook

The play opened sensationally. The Englishmen got in passing rushes, and were looking dangerous, when Thomas, with his back to goal, tried to centre with an overhead punt, but misjudged and kicked towards his own goal, he let in Australia disastrously. The ball went beyond the visiting full-back, and was secured by Farnsworth, who was well attended by comrades and there was but one Englishman. Fearing an attack from behind, Farnsworth passed to Hickey, who scored a try, which Messenger converted. Australia 5 England nil.

The next score was credited to England and was a try, which came from a dual between dribblers. The ball was worked by the toe over the line, and Leytham fell on it. Lomas failed at goal. Australia, 5 to 3... The ball was slung about in all directions, until in front of England's goal the play was stopped by one of the touch-judges and he reported a case of illegal interference. From the resultant free-kick Messenger kicked the goal amidst much enthusiasm. Australia 7 to 3.

The game was fast and the combination by each side was beautifully executed, the visitors being rather more graceful in their work than their opponents, each man running into his position at a gallop. The referee was strict, and there were many penalties.

...Then a great bit of work came. Sullivan initiated a series of passes, in which the ball was handled by several light blues. The defence was weakened by the absence of Sharrock, who had just been placed *hors de combat*. Close to the line the transfer went to Messenger, who, running round, eluded an opponent, and planted the ball behind the goal. He also converted. Australia 12 to 3.

Points were now put up at a rare pace. Brilliant work enabled Thomas to score a try, which Lomas with a great kick, converted, and a few moments passing by the threequarters, closed with a try by Leytham, the kick for goal failing. Half-time: Australia 12 England 11. Sharrock had not been able to resume his place.

A gloom was cast over the crowd by the removal of Sharrock on a stretcher. He had tried to walk, and collapsed. His lip was cut, and he was suffering from concussion.

Second half

Australia attacked from the kick-off, and looked dangerous, when an intercept pass completely changed the scene to the home line. A free-kick relieved the pressure for a moment, but then came a beautiful passing movement by England, which closed with a try by Jukes, which was unconverted. This placed England in the lead by 14 points to Australia's 12... the Englishmen were playing a great game, and superior to Australia...

Sharrock here returned to the game, and unanimous and great applause greeted his appearance, for it was feared he had been dangerously hurt.

England's next score came from a brilliant effort and one that was initiated by the great Lomas. He took the ball from a Light Blue [Australian] close to the touchline in his own half and ran. Then followed clean and remarkably clever passing, which ended in Jukes scoring close to goal, and Lomas converted. England 19 to 12.

It was now Australia's turn to do something great. From 25 to 25 the ball was taken by a series of passes all more or less interfered with by the tackling of the visitors. Still the rush continued and, during it there were many cries of "They're in" but they were not. The defence of the visitors was superb, though on one occasion it seemed the referee should have allowed a mark for a catch by a Light Blue at close quarters just in front of goal. The excitement was intense, and the crowd showed their disapproval by hooting, which was repeated presently when the referee allowed a mark to an Englishman. This mark led to yet another try by Jukes, and a conversion by Lomas. England 24 to 12. It was always Lomas. Here he opened the way to a try by Batten. The English captain failed at goal. England 27 to 12. Hickey was the next Australian to score. With only the full-back to block him the ball was passed to Spence, who ran behind the posts. Messenger converted. England 27 to 17. Within a moment Australia were in again, Woodhead getting over after magnificent play. The kick for goal failed. England 27 Australia 20. Full time."

Many reporters and supporters believed that the Australians were not on their game. The reason could have been that they were more affected by the aftermath of Wednesday's game than the Northern Union. If that were the case then Mr Sherwood, the chief police officer for Sydney, could truly be said to have won the first test for the Northern Union without kicking a ball. Frank Bickford was sarcastic in his report in the *Oldham Chronicle* on Wednesday 3 August: "Referee McMahon was in charge, and under his stark rule there was no manifestation of ill-feeling. Quite the other way. Both teams were beastly polite – too polite in fact! Did an Australian grass a man, he shook hands on the ground and helped his man up. Did an Englishman bowl an Australian halfway into the following week, he considerately caught him and hauled him back again to his proper place in the calendar. But in spite of this charming spirit a couple of Englishmen got laid out. Sharrock, the full-back, suffered from a slight concussion and was carried off on a stretcher. Later on Ward was seen rolling about the field in agony, and he too was carried off."

Maybe the Australians only played as well as the tourists let them. This was a game worthy of a test match and for some reason does not get the credit it deserves in this country.

Perhaps the sport's followers are more familiar with the NU victory in the famous Rorke's Drift test match on the 1914 tour. This match saw the Northern Union play for much of the time with only 12 men, Sharrock was badly concussed after a collision with a number of Australian forwards. In the second half, for a time they were down to 11 men while Ward was off receiving treatment along with Sharrock who was off for running repairs. It was a magnificent win for the tourists who were still only three weeks into the tour.

James Lomas had a tremendous game in both attack and defence, and led his men not only with great skill, but also by example. According to the reports whenever Lomas had the ball in hand the crowd thought he was likely to score. It seems he even outplayed the Australians' favourite son, Dally Messenger, and for the press to acknowledge that was high praise indeed. In fairness, no one took a backward step all afternoon for the Northern Union.

On Wednesday 22 June the *Sydney Sportsman* suggested that the crowd was nearer to 42,000 plus and wrote that "by two o' clock the spectators were fighting for seats". The reporter went on to say: "There was not the slightest doubt that the... previous Wednesday [the Metropolis match] was a marvellous advertisement for this game, thousands coming in the hope of a repetition of that day's mix-up, and if they were disappointed in this respect, they found themselves fully compensated in the strenuous and stirring display that was served up to them.

"Mr Clifford, the NU manager, may be credited to a great extent with the clean and sportsmanlike way the test game was played, as he visited both teams in their dressing room, and delivered to each a stirring lecture, telling the players among other things, that they had practically the fate of the League in their hands that day – meaning that a recurrence of Wednesday's discreditable performance would be the death knell of the Northern Union game in Australia.

"Judging by the manner the 26 players ultimately conducted themselves, the words of Mr Clifford sank in deeply, and all League enthusiasts were delighted to see everything go off smartly..."

What would the reaction be today to a tour manager visiting both dressing rooms before a game and telling them how they should play the game?

James Leytham, ever a modest man, made only the briefest of mentions in his diary when he wrote: "...it turned out one of the best games ever played in Australia and England won by 27 points to 20. The scorers were Jukes 3 tries, Leytham 2 tries, Batten 1 try Thomas 1 try, Lomas 3 goals..."

That was all he said about the game. What was not in doubt was that the first test had been won, and won by the tourists who had come good at just the right time.

One other interesting point was the behaviour of Messenger as the game came to its conclusion. The Australians had scored a try at the death to take the score to 27–20. Messenger strode up to take the simple conversion – after teeing up the ball, he ran up and simply tapped the ball forward, making no attempt to convert. He then raced after the rolling ball and picked it up, knowing full well the game was over. By doing so he secured the ball – a momentous souvenir from the first ever Australia versus England test played in Australia, the match ball.

After this match, one of the tourists, the injured Leeds full-back, Frank Young, who had not travelled to Newcastle, wrote to his club. He described the battle that was raging between the two codes in Sydney. He wrote: "The Rugby Union and Northern Union here are fighting like dogs against each other, but the professional game is all the rage. In Sydney, New South Wales Rugby Union played New Zealand on the cricket ground and we played in the next field. It was comical to notice how their spectators stuck their heads over the cricket ground rails to watch our game when they had paid to watch the other. It does not matter who you speak to in Sydney, they are all for the Northern Union game."

While he may well have been biased, Young was simply reflecting the attitude of many Sydney folk at this time. The first test between the two countries further strengthened the position of the league game over the union code in the city.

Bert Avery, in a letter back to Oldham, published in the *Chronicle* on 25 July, referred to the first test in a similar vein: "At the Sydney Cricket Ground which is the next field to where we played, the NSW universities were playing the Americans followed by the Maori v NSW Amateurs and [they] could only command a gate of 12,000 so you can see which game is taken on best."

The celebrations on winning the first test were a bit muted because half the party were already in Newcastle. On Monday 20 June, the tourists made their way along George Street to the railway station and at 9am boarded the train for Newcastle. They arrived at Newcastle around 1pm and went to their hotel to join the rest of the party. Now they were all together the official welcome to Newcastle could get underway. They went to a reception at the Town Hall hosted by the mayor and in the evening were invited to a smoking concert by the Newcastle District Rugby League.

On the Tuesday before the match they were given the day off and as Leytham noted: "...We went on the beach to have a bathe in a place called The Bogey Hole, which the convicts cut out of solid rock and we had a look round the asylum. We also went down a coal pit called Sea Pit. We went down through a tunnel to a depth of about 285 feet and the seam of coal was 13 feet thick, we walked all the way through straight up."

Having played the second game in Newcastle on the Wednesday and won comfortably 40–20 there was yet again little time to celebrate. Leytham wrote: "We left Newcastle at 8.40pm. On 22nd June and got out of the train on 23rd June at 10.30 at night, that was 25½ hour ride, [but] we did have a sleeper."

Today the world is seen as a small place, things have not changed much from Leytham's day for he wrote about that train journey from Newcastle to Brisbane: "I met a man from Lancaster related to Banks Thompson the old Lancaster forward."

Leytham had been signed by Wigan from Lancaster and probably played with or knew of the player mentioned. His diary continued: "We arrived [in] Brisbane and a large crowd was there and gave us three cheers and then drove to Carlton Club Hotel where we had a good reception and then was ready for our own beds. Next day we had our photographs taken, which I am going to have. In the afternoon we went to the Town Hall and [were] received by the Mayor of Brisbane and we had a lovely reception. It is a lovely place."

While they were in Brisbane the players were told of an extra match that had been arranged on the Monday following their forthcoming match against Queensland. The original intention had been to follow the same preparation as in Sydney. They would play on the first Saturday and the following Wednesday against a Queensland side and on the second Saturday play the second test in Brisbane. However, Monday 27 June had been declared a public holiday to celebrate the Prince of Wales's birthday and Clifford and Houghton in their wisdom agreed to play an extra match on that day. The problem was, the tourists were in Brisbane, the extra match was scheduled to be played back in Sydney, more than 700 miles away.

The match was to be played against the Kangaroos – players who were members of the 1908–09 tour to Great Britain. This match was arranged to give the Australian players a chance of making some money from their share of the gate and was a match the tourists were unlikely to win. It did, however, offer the prospect of another good gate and more income. Clifford and Houghton never lost sight of the fact that the tour really needed to make a profit for the Northern Union. Once again their instincts proved correct as the match attracted a crowd of more than 30,000, according to the *Herald*. The players never seemed to find either the travelling or the extra matches a problem, or if they did they did not complain. In those times, while the captain may well have been king on the field, off it, it was the managers who held sway. What they said went and was not questioned.

Leytham wrote: "We left Brisbane on Sunday morning to go to Sydney to play an extra match versus [the] Kangaroos. [It was] a holiday for the Prince of Wales's birthday and we lost by 22 to 10. We were all knocked up by the travelling 700 miles. On our way we saw two large flocks of cattle with two cowboys to each lot going right through the bush and also saw some polo on horseback being played. We had good sleeping cars and plenty of good food to eat, turkey, chicken... We travelled 1,400 miles in 60 hours, had five hours to play a match and rest, so that was not much. We arrived back on Tuesday June 26th very tired, day after we were invited to look round a biscuit factory..."

75

Even the reporters accepted that defeat was inevitable given the travel schedule the tourists faced. *The Herald* reported on 28 June: "The Englishmen were tired after their trip from the northern state, otherwise they would have sustained their earlier efforts and rendered a better account of themselves."

Bert Avery, in a letter published on 10 August in Oldham, showed the lighter side of the players' attitude to the long distances travelled: "We had a spiffing return journey, having two sleeping saloons to ourselves. We meant to take things easy after the rush down, and we did. Mr Houghton did not make the return journey with us, having to fix up the arrangements for our trip New Zealand and also for the return journey. He, however, instituted Johnny Thomas and Curzon to look after us, and we soon christened them 'Young Houghton' and 'Young Clifford'. The party having two saloons, was, of course, divided, so to make things enjoyable we decided to name each saloon after a theatre and have a sing song sort of thing. Our saloon was called the 'Theatre Royal' and the other the 'Palace'. Boylen started the entertainment in one, and in theatrical language 'he got the bird', and he was fired out into the other theatre, where he met with no better reception and was bundled back in quick time. We had a rare good time I can tell you - not half! Turkey [for] breakfast - not bad, eh?..."

On the Wednesday some of the players had to turn out again, this time against Queensland. It was not really the best preparation for the second test, although the tourists won comfortably 15–4, scoring five tries against two goals for the home side.

Everything was now set up for the second test match. Australia needed to win to level the series, while the NU merely needed to draw to retain the Ashes. As the Saturday dawned, all the players were ready, as were the Brisbane public. Rugby union in Queensland had quickly realised that they could not compete with this game. They were due to host a local cup final on the same day but, fearing the match would be played in an almost empty stadium, they rearranged it for the following weekend when the tourists would have left the area.

The weather was almost perfect for playing rugby. It was warm and sunny and the pitch was in good condition. All they wanted was a fair crack of the whip from the match officials. It is interesting to note that the rivalry between New South Wales and Queensland in the State of Origin series was present in the press. The newspapers talked of the maroon and light blue of the Australian shirts whereas their Sydney counterparts reversed the colours in their reports.

76

The Second test

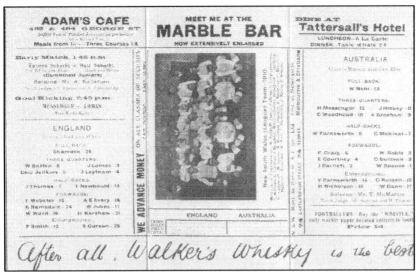

The teams from the match programme.
(Courtesy Don Hammond, NZRL Museum)

The goalkicking contest before the game – James Lomas kicks for goal.
(Courtesy Rob Deller)

The NU players were becoming more and more upset with the way in which referees were interpreting the rules. They could not understand how, after 15 years of playing the game, they seemed to get on the wrong side of officials who only had two or three years experience of the same rules.

Avery wrote at the end of the Australian leg of the tour in the *Chronicle* on 3 September: "You will perhaps have heard that they say [Australian press] we are always talking and arguing with the referee, and well we might! Some of them are quite novices at the rules, but, of course you cannot expect them to be experts yet. Only they seem to think they are in the right."

The two teams took to the field on that Saturday afternoon in front of around 18,000 spectators, one of the largest if not the largest crowd to witness any rugby match in Queensland at that time.

The Australians had made wholesale changes from the first match. In Sydney there had only been one Queensland player in the test team. Now, in Brisbane, the team boasted seven from that state and Bill Heidke, a Queenslander, was installed as captain. The teams were:
Australia: D. McGregor, C. Woodhead, J.J. Hickey, H.H. Messenger, W. Heidke, W. Farnsworth, C.H. McKivat, E. Buckley, H. Nicholson, J.T. Barnett, R. Tubman, R. Craig, H. Brackenreg.
England: J. Sharrock, W. Batten, J. Lomas, J. Riley, J. Leytham, J. Thomas, F. Smith, F. Webster, W. Winstanley, H. Kershaw, R. Ramsdale, W. Jukes, G. Ruddick.
Referee: Mr J. Fihelly.

Before the match there was a goalkicking contest between Dally Messenger, Jim Lomas and Herb Brackenreg. Brackenreg won, scoring twice to Messenger's once. Lomas missed all three of his attempts.

The reporter in the *Brisbane Courier* was perhaps not as flowing in his praise of the tourists as was his Sydney counterpart. He wrote:

England versus Australia 2nd Test
The Australian team led by their captain W. Heidke, took the field first and were joined immediately by the Englishmen. After an exchange of cheers the teams took up their positions, the Englishmen playing from the stand end of the ground. Brackenreg for Australia sent the ball well to the English wing, it was returned to midfield, where Messenger picked up and ran a few yards, and then with a beautiful kick, sent the ball behind the posts from the drop. Many of the spectators thought that a field goal had been scored, but no points were allowed. From the kick-off England forced play. Eventually play worked back across

the field and up to England's territory. Here Buckley secured at the '25' but was captured immediately. He handed out to Woodward, who dived for the line, but was brought down within a yard of it. He did not lose the ball, however, but passed quickly to Barnett, who was just in time. Brackenreg failed a goal. Australia 3 England 0.

During the next bout of play the most noticeable feature was the kicking of Brackenreg and Messenger. Finally out on the wing Messenger picked up when the ball was at his opponent's feet, and with a clear field before him ran over. Brackenreg's attempt at goal was a failure. Australia 6 England 0.

The enthusiasm of the crowd at this point reached its height, and the spectators cheered almost continually as Australia again commenced to gain ground. In a ruck McKivat secured and scored between the posts, Hickey converting easily. Australia 11 England 0.

From a scrum near midway on the wing the Englishmen worked the ball out towards the grandstand and a series of rapid passes placed it in the hands of Lomas, who, accompanied by Leytham made a fierce onslaught, and broke through the Australian line. Then the ball was transferred to Leytham, who scored, Lomas converted. Australia 11 England 5.

At about 3.55pm, before the close of the half England gained her second try after one of the most magnificent rushes of the whole afternoon... The ball was set in motion at midway, and in a moment the whole field was bunched and moving at top speed, the Australian forwards being mostly on the outer wing from the stand. A second later Webster came into view with the ball. About 10 yards from the line he gave to Thomas, who, working in a little towards the posts placed down conveniently. Lomas added the extra points. The half time came a minute later, with the scores: Australia 11 England 10.

Early in the second half the play worked towards England's goal, but Thomas relieved the position, and breaking through the pack, made a daring run, coming out in front of the Australian posts. Messenger brought him down, picked up, dodged and Englishman, sidestepped another and executed a similar movement immediately afterwards. Then seeing himself in difficulties, he kicked coolly down field. At mid-field the next minute he was again in possession and was tackled hard by Ramsdale. Both players fell, and remained on the ground, Messenger apparently suffering acute pain. He was removed from the field by the Ambulance Brigade. In the face of this calamity the crowd scarcely noticed that a try had been scored by Kershaw, thus placing England in the lead. Lomas hit the post with his kick, no points of course being given.

After the restart Messenger resumed his place on the field, although suffering a great deal of inconvenience. It was not long before England added another three through the agency of Leytham, but no goal points were gained.

From this [point] onward the Englishmen gave a good deal of trouble to the referee. On more than one occasion they questioned his decision. Up to this point Mr Fihelly had been very lenient, but after two free kicks had been allowed against them for rough play, he ordered Ruddick off. Lomas protested, but Mr Fihelly was firm, and the player left the field. Thereafter the play improved.

On resuming Leytham picked up on the wing near the '25' and placed down behind the posts. Thomas failed at goal. Australia 11 England 19.

An electric run by Messenger from midfield almost to the English line, and another dash by the Australian backs, which was initiated by the same player, lent interest to the next period of play. The last move by the Australians proved disastrous, as it happened, for the English got possession and carried the ball right back to the Australian section of the field. Here Jukes passed to Leytham who successfully contested a long run with McGregor, and added another try to the British list. He did not succeed in converting his own score.

A series of passing rushes by Australia led to a try by Craig, of New South Wales, which remained unconverted. Australia appeared to be thoroughly awake now and their passing rushes were such as we have rarely seen in Queensland. At one point when the ball was in the midfield, Buckley gave to Brackenreg, who negotiated a dodgy run, working in towards the dressing sheds and finally gave to Hickey, who was swamped, the ball going to ground where Nicholson secured and ran over. Messenger failed at goal. Australia 17 England 22

The play continued very exciting, and a moment before the whistle sounded a scrum was given exactly on the Australian goal line. The closing scores were: England 22 Australia 17."

The Northern Union players were more than a stone a man heavier than their rivals. This weight difference was much more pronounced in the backs where the tourists' threequarter line was far heavier than the opposition. Such an advantage inevitably told as the match wore on. Even so, yet again, the tourists played part of the match with only

12 men on the field, although this time due to a sending off and not an injury.

So the tourists had completed what they set out to do, and won the test series. What they also did in those two matches was to record achievements which stand even to this day. Billy Jukes, the Hunslet forward, scored a hat-trick in the first test. It is a feat which has not been beaten since by a forward. In the second test, James Leytham crossed for four tries. He is still the only player to score four tries in a test between the two countries to this day. Leytham, in his diary, made little reference to the game or his own feats when he wrote: "The day of the second test match. England won 22 to 17, so we have won the rubber. I scored four tries in this match. We have a lot of trouble with the referee every match..."

After all, scoring four or more tries in a match was not unusual for Leytham, he had done so for Wigan on a number of occasions. He referred to the Mr Fihelly's refereeing. After the match the referee apologised and admitted he was wrong to send Ruddick from the field. The tourists' problems with match officials were not going away.

The other problem might well have been one of keeping interest alive in the rest of the tour, as there seemed little to play for now the series was won. Nothing could have been further from the truth. There was another match that the public were looking forward to with equal anticipation to that which they had shown for the test series. The tourists were due to meet Australasia in Sydney. It was a contest between the old country and the new colonies.

The press was already referring to it as a match between the Northern and Southern Hemispheres to see who would dominate the game. The public lapped up the prospect and it became pivotal in league's battle with union for the hearts and minds of the Australian public. It was on that day, 9 July 1910, that the New South Wales rugby union were finally forced to concede they could no longer compete with the Northern Unionists.

For that reason that game turned out to be perhaps the most important in the early history of the league code in Australia. Most certainly it captured the imagination of the whole of the country and also New Zealand for that matter.

It is difficult to say just when or how it was decided to play a second game against Australasia, but play it they did. That match, on Wednesday 13 July, was expected to be the last match in Australia on the tour.

However, as always on this tour, such matters were flexible and a further match in Sydney was arranged for the tourists after the New Zealand leg was completed. The tourists had to return to Sydney to board the ship for home, so why waste the opportunity of playing in another match and another potentially coffer-swelling gate?

6. Australasia

There has been a myth in the history of this tour that the Australasia match was arranged to replace a third test between the NU and Australia, which would have had little attraction after the tourists won the first two tests.

It would make sense that the authorities would seek to replace a meaningless game with one that was more attractive and could draw a large crowd. What better then than to have a combined Australia and New Zealand side? The truth is somewhat different. The *Evening Post* in New Zealand carried a small article on 18 June which had been sent by telegram the previous day. It read:

Six League men wanted
"Mr Watts, secretary of the New Zealand Rugby League, has received a cablegram from Sydney to the effect that the match Britain V Australasia had been fixed for 9 July, and asking that six New Zealanders be sent, three backs and three forwards. The men will be chosen by the selectors at an early date."

This cablegram was sent five days prior to the second test. So unless the authorities were psychic or expected Australia to lose why would they want six New Zealand players to travel over? The answer is simple – the match had always been intended to be played on 9 July.

There was a week to prepare for the game against the combined Australia and New Zealand team. The tourists had to get back to Sydney, while the Australasian team had to assemble and practice. The selectors had chosen only two New Zealand players to augment the team. Full-back Riki Papakura and wingman Albert 'Opai' Asher had to be integrated into the squad once they arrived from New Zealand. They did not do so until late in the week and, when they did, both were a little under the weather. The four day crossing had been a rough one and both suffered from sea-sickness.

As has been discussed, the war between the two codes in Australia had all but come to an end, or had at least arrived at an uneasy truce. There was the occasional skirmish along the way and snipes at the professionals by the old guard but that was the limit of it. What the tour had achieved was to cement the Northern Union code and its values into the sporting psyche of the Australian public. This has lasted until today. Most rugby league historians would agree that if there was one game in the whole tour which finally convinced the rugby union leadership that the battle had been lost, it was the first clash between Australasia and the Northern Union.

To the union officials, such a match was of no significance, they could not see the relevance of it. The two test matches they could understand, but this artificial, contrived fixture, what possible interest could it have for Sydney folk? They were about to find out in a very emphatic manner.

The build up to the game was taken very seriously by both sides. The combined Australian and New Zealand team saw it as a chance to salvage something from the tour, a chance to avenge the test defeats. The press saw it as a clash between the northern and southern hemispheres for the right to claim who were the top dogs in the Northern Union game. The tourists, on the other hand, must have found it difficult to lift themselves. They had completed the job they came to do, win the Ashes, now they had to gather momentum once more to meet a combined side, which they did. Leytham wrote in his diary: "...We arrived back in Sydney on 4 July at 11.30 in the morning so we rested for the rest of the day. The day after we went into training again and also went down to Bronte for a swim. The day after we had sports – ¼ mile race. Farrar came in first but a lot did not try. 15 shillings was the first prize, it was to get them all to turn out together. We have had two hours every day training and [we] go swimming in the afternoon.

"On 6 July we were invited to the Naval depot where all of the sailors sleep at night, the place was within a few yards of were the first flag was hoisted in Australia and we had a pleasant evening. Each player got with six sailors round a table, they were Welshmen, Irishmen, Yorkshire and Lancashire men. One chap from Wigan called Frank Heath, a stoker, was on a boat called Prometheus.

"We have been in strict training for our match with Australasia on July 9 where we expect a large crowd."

In the week preceding the game the tourists had been invited to attend a dinner at the docks. Their hosts were the British Navy, a number of ships having arrived in the city within the last week. Bert Avery in a letter home provides an insight, just as Leytham had, of the rugby fever that had gripped Sydney on this last week of the tour: "Last Wednesday night we were entertained in splendid fashion by the men of the navy at the Royal Navy House here. The enthusiasm throughout the proceedings was great, and the affair was one which will long remain in our memories.

The Blue Jackets expressed a desire that they should be allowed to pull the 'drag' with us on board from our hotel to the ground on the occasion of our match versus Australasia on the following Saturday. Our managers tried to put them off, but they were persistent and it was agreed they should pull the 'drag' into the ground and around the field which they did..."

Leytham described their arrival at the ground: "They [the sailors] took the horses out and pulled us round the field with a band in front, cheer after cheer went up. When the whistle blew for time they all rushed on the ground and carried us off to the dressing room and waited for us. They took the horses out again and pulled us to our hotel. It was a great sight watching them."

It is not clear if the management had any idea just how important this game really was. Some of the press were referring to it as a test between the mother country and the new colonies. Whatever the newspapers said, it seemed not to matter, this encounter had gripped the imagination of Sydney's rugby followers.

As the day of the Australasia match dawned, people were already making their way toward the Agricultural Society Showground at Moore Park. However, the venue was really not big enough for the crowd. There was always a tendency to overestimate attendances at matches by the local press. The attendance which is printed in the papers for this game of 50,000 is probably an overestimate, because the showground at that time simply could not accommodate a crowd of that size. The true attendance was probably nearer to 43,000. If the Sydney Cricket Ground had been available the attendance would have topped the 52,000 that attended a rugby union test between Australian and New Zealand a few years earlier. The Australian rugby union had a lease on the ground to play union and simply refused to allow the league game to be played there.

The tourists certainly expected a gate similar to the one that had seen the first test match. Bert Avery wrote: "Saturday turned out fine with a bit of breeze up. The rest of the players other than those selected had to leave the hotel at 11 o'clock in the morning to be on the gates as there was a big crowd expected and I am pleased to say everything turned out according to expectations for when the teams arrived at 2.30 there were fully 40,000 on the ground."

This would suggest that the tourists, while not manning the turnstiles, were at least monitoring that all the gates were manned and turnstiles working. More importantly, they ensured that everyone entering the ground was actually paying to do so. The players were very aware just how important it was that the tour made a profit. Avery also gave a more reasonable assessment of the crowd attending the match than the local reporters.

Such was the importance of this match and the consequences for the game in Australia that the whole day is best described by the reporter of the *Sydney Sportsman*. In the edition of Wednesday 13 July they devoted a whole page to the event.

Australasia versus England

Out at the Agricultural Ground the mighty multitude surged. For hours before the "meeting of the giants" just one continuous stream of people flowed through the clicking turnstiles, and the silver pattered into the League moneyboxes even as the rain patters down in a summer shower. The faces of secretary Larkin and the League officials fairly beamed with joy and satisfaction, the barrackers for the new game were jubilant and took every opportunity of drawing the attention of all Union barrackers they happened to tumble across, to the magnificent turn up. It was like rubbing it in; but seemingly they were unable to resist the opportunity."

The writer described the entrance of the NU players with the blue jackets. He continued: "Everything had been beautifully arranged. A thunder of applause greeted them. Hard upon their heels came the Australasians, so called on account of having in their ranks the crack of New South Wales and Queensland a brace of Maorilanders in the persons of Ashley and Papakura. Never before has the writer witnessed such excitement amongst a football multitude as the men files into position on the field. For the first time in the week the Johnson-Jeffries sensation appeared to be forgotten, interest was centred upon the local men as if the fate of the nation depended upon them winning. Then captain Lomas kicked off and the fun began.

"Summing up, the match was not a dazzling one from a spectators' point of view. There was certainly meteoric flashes and a few passing rushes which caused the spectators to rise up and whoop like so many lunatics but rushes of that kind were too few and far between. All the time the tackling was too swift and deadly to repeat the passing rushes which bring such joy to the heart of the onlookers... From the kick-off to the final toot of the referees whistle each side played 'all out'. The forwards sustained a pace which was simply stupendous and the backs were all as alert and quick as cats. But the tackling was a feature. Gee! It was deadly determined all the time, without exception in a few instances – being vicious.

"Up to halfway through the second half it appeared as if the Englishmen were about to meet their Waterloo. But they appeared to suddenly pull themselves together and attacking like tigers had the Australasians battling in the defence as if for dear life. The visitors were not to be denied though and bursting through in gallant style finally evened up the score. As they stood at the end and the ball went up and down the field of play again the excitement rose to fever heat. But although our men made desperate attempts to again score and the Englishmen in turn sought strenuously to cross the line, the sun went down on a drawn game...

"It was a memorable day for the Rugby League and a match combined with a display which must have won to its ranks thousands of adherents. Very few begrudged the Englishmen the pleasurable satisfaction of having succeeded in pulling the match out of the fire and making a drawn game of it. Their puck and pertinacity backed up by brilliant play, fully entitled them to all they earned.

In the evening the teams and the officials of League breasted the banqueting board at Margretta. A glance around the festive board discovered an array of splendid specimens of manly and muscular young giants. Many of them had lost stripes of steak off their beauteous dials and all were in a fearful good humour. And made the chicken, roast duck and lager fly away in phenomenal fashion. It was very festive, with the band playing and the boys all keeping time by roaring out popular choruses with time, the glasses and dishes clattering merrily.

The president, the bejewelled Joynton Smith, was first to rise up to speak on the occasion. He flirted with a silvery tenor voice whilst posed in an attitude which would have filled even Julius Knight with envy. He fired off many platitudes-well worn-ones regarding our athletes of today being our main defenders against the invading enemy of tomorrow. He also got some fairly good horse sense off his chest regarding the manner in which the stars of the League had risen, and its future chances of shining with undiminished lustre. He refrained from pelting the Union with quicklime in the hour of triumph as the League was now in such a position that the scarifying of the opposition faction was totally unnecessary. He made many flowery remarks to the visitors and pointed out that the teeball honore so far in their favour. He extended to the local lads a fatherly pat on the back for the splendour of their performance and finally sat down with a beaming smile and a flash of diamond shirt stud amidst much applause."

The writer then looked at the performances of the players: "Dick Papakura wasn't nearly the same old 'Pap' that put up the marvellous games when the Maoris were over here; but he had only arrived on Friday night, after a rough passage and was sea sick the whole day.

Opal Asher was in his glory when he found the Britishers were willing to muck up, and lost all interest in the winning of the game in his desire to have a crack at the last one who had passed him one.

Messenger's game was the best he has given us since his return to form and he made some of the opposition look dead sheep on a number of occasions. Viv Farnworth was good and got a bonser try; but to my mind didn't come nearly up to Darb Hickey and was too much inclined to go on his own.

Broomham was a treat and although he didn't score, he hardly made a mistake, and runs with a marvellous strength for one of his weight. Billy Farnsworth has played better games this season and the dose of Dally's 'speedy oil' he took before the game didn't liven him up much. Chrissy Mac played Aunt Sally in his best form, especially in the second half, when the home team was getting the 'puddan'.

The forwards were a very even lot, with Cann and Courtney showing out most prominently. Cann got the hots about every two minutes with his vis-à-vis on the end of the scrum, and looking like Ajax defying the lightening as the referee gave him some tender words of advice.

England's full-back Sharrock was solid but a trifle slower than previously. Batten couldn't go right and something went wrong every time the ball came his way and what with India rubber Asher opposite him, he had a very unhappy time of it.

Lomas wanted to win on his own and spoilt several good opportunities by hanging on and he has never kicked worse out here. By the way he ought to handcuff that dirty left of his when he tackles. It had a bad habit of bobbing into the tackled ones dial, to the latter's great discomfort. Jenkins did all that was asked of him, and kept his wingman fed. Leytham got the lion's share of the ball on the wing, and frisked about like a three year old.

The two halves were the pick of the back division, and worked like Trojans right through. Jukes, Webster and Avery were the pick of the forwards, but Avery would do well to shut the phonograph off when he is playing. It is a wonder he doesn't get hoarse with the constant chirping."

The teams were:

Australasia: Papakura (NZ), Asher (NZ), Messenger (NSW – capt.), V. Farnsworth (NSW), Broomham (NSW), W. Farnsworth (NSW), McKivat (NSW), Brackenreg (Q), Courtney (NSW), Pearce (NSW), Craig (NSW), Cann (NSW) Sullivan (NSW)

England: J. Sharrock, W. Batten, J. Lomas (capt), B. Jenkins, J. Leytham, J. Thomas, T.H. Newbould, F. Webster, W. Winstanley, H. Kershaw, R. Ramsdale, W. Jukes, A.E. Avery,

Referee: Tom McMahon

The reporter's description of the play was as follows:

"Messenger won the toss and played with the wind, which was blowing in spiteful gusts and a great assistance although the team had a blinding sun in their eyes. England's kick off went out of touch on the full and the ball was scrummed in the centre...

Give and take play ensued for a few minutes... Viv Farnsworth came clean through the ruck and set sail for the line, and although tackled, he had enough way on to force himself over, and Australasia draw first blood Messenger missed the goal. Australasia 3 England 0...

England by keeping the ball low soon got dangerous, and Asher being hard-pressed deliberately knocked on to save his side, and a free kick was given to England. Lomas made no mistake. Australasia 3 England 2.

Australasia livened up after this score and had England in an awkward position. Sharrock got blocked under the bar and kicked down field but the ball struck a squall, and Sandy Pearce marked in a handy position, and his club mate Dally M landed an easy goal. Australasia 5 England 2.

Broomham who was putting up a slashing game as usual, now got busy and did a couple of tricky runs down the boundary, but deadly tackling prevented a score. From a cross kick Messenger came from the clouds, and with one of his hare like runs made a beautiful opening for Courtney and smiling Ned lobbed across dead easy, Brackenreg missed an easy goal. Australasia 8, England 2.

Papakura was, up to this stage, playing very disappointingly, but the sun in his eyes made the taking of the ball very difficult. His fellow NZ rep. Asher was also having a pretty bad time on the wing, the ball very rarely coming his way. When it did, the bounce generally beat him, but getting possession once, he lit out in a hurry, and Batten was the most surprised man on the ground as he grabbed a handful of atmosphere when Asher did one of his beautiful sensational jumps clean over him. He only gained 10 yards more when he was pushed out of bounds, tearing and scraping to the delight of the huge crowd.

"England now pulled themselves together, and inch by inch with solid ruck work they got well into the Blues' territory... Newbould got his backs going, and when the leather came to Leytham he had a clear sprint for the corner, which he reached successfully, and to the surprise of everyone never tried to better his position for goalkicking purposes.

"A big majority of the spectators thought that Leytham took this pass offside, but, from the writer's position it was perfectly correct, and the whole passing bout thoroughly deserved the success it attained. Lomas missed the goal. Australasia 8 England 5...

"When the teams appeared again [for the second half] the strong breeze had dropped considerably, which made the home team's task a lot easier...

"From the kick-off England started an attack, but one of the threequarters miss-kicked and Broomham getting held did a feinting run alone the line, and, when blocked, passed to the ever ready Billy Cann, who side-stepped a treat and cut for the line, with no one in front of him, and when a score looked certain, John Thomas took him behind and grassed him a few inches from the line...

A penalty against the visitors gave Messenger an opportunity that he availed himself of and he landed a good goal. Australasia 10 England 5.

After Lomas had had a shot for goal which went wide, the Blues got off the mark again and Broomham gave young Chris McKivat a pass and the curly kid made no error, no goal resulting. Australasia 13 England 5...

From a broken scrum Avery picked up, and the Blues standing off him expecting him to pass, let him right through in the most simple fashion and he got across in a good position, and to the spectators surprise Lomas missed an easy goal.

Australasia 13, England 8

From now on, to the finish the home team had a red hot time defending, the Red and Whites being in their 25 nearly all of the time. The only time Australasia looked like scoring was when Messenger intercepted and, like a flash, was up the field with only the full-back to pass. With the solid game he had been playing Dally was pretty well winded when he reached Sharrock, and did the best thing under the circumstances – punted over the latter's head, but before Messenger could reach the ball in rolled out of bounds.

The Englishmen were not long in bringing the leather back again and Winstanley raised the English score by bumping his way over and Lomas converted. Australasia 13 England 13..."

An interesting aspect of the match was the play of the New Zealand wingman Albert Opai Asher. A feature of his play involved him, on approaching a would-be tackler in waiting until the last possible moment. Then, as the tackler stooped, Asher would leap over the top of him rather like a hurdler. Asher beat Batten this way, but was tackled just 10 yards further down the field. It was a move Batten himself used, so he should not have been surprised. It was also one his son, Eric Batten, would use to good effect when he played at the top level, until the move was deemed to be very dangerous and outlawed by the RFL.

There is no doubt that it was this one encounter and the large size of the crowd it attracted that finally brought home to rugby union's leadership that financially they could no longer compete with the Northern Union. The battles had been won and now the war had been won. The resulting loss was to see rugby union never recover in Australia. Even today rugby league still holds sway in both Queensland and New South Wales. It still holds that ascendancy in spite of competition from association football, rugby union and Aussie Rules. It was this one encounter that ensured complete victory for the game.

The other interesting thing about the match report was that on the same page was a cartoon. It was a direct reference to the comment made at the beginning of the tour by an unnamed rugby union official, who stated to the press that they [the Rugby Union] would play before empty stands rather than go down the professional route. The statement came back to haunt him and rugby union as the press took on board what he had said and applied it in the context of just how successful the tour had been and the damage it had done to the old game. The cartoon depicted a rugby union match being played in front of an almost empty stand. If that were not enough, the cartoon carried under it a poem poking fun at the attitude of the rugby union

There can be little doubt as to which code of rugby *The Sydney Sportsman* was in favour of. The cartoon ran under the headline: "The hot air from a Union football official" and said "A promise which looks like a prophecy – 'We shall play to empty benches rather than jeopardise our amateur status.'"

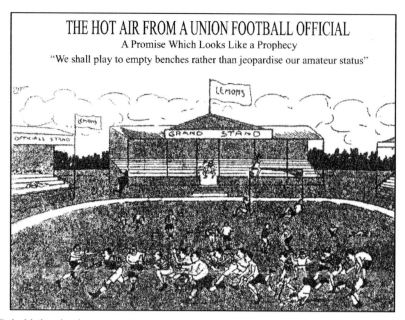

THE HOT AIR FROM A UNION FOOTBALL OFFICIAL
A Promise Which Looks Like a Prophecy
"We shall play to empty benches rather than jeopardise our amateur status"

Behold the day has come to pass,
It seems so, well we know;
The benches that were spoken of,
Are sadly empty now.

The players still they nobly stick,
And play the game right fast.
But with no crowd to cheer them on,
Say, how long will they last?

The old traditions senseless now,
Aye, sadly out of date.
As men within the union ranks
Are finding out too late.

They've slumbered long, rode the high horse
Their 'guiding star' now see
They've simply lived within a state
Of false security.

Behold the empty benches now,
So filled in days of yore.
There's just a fat man in the stands,
And don't you hear him snore?

Officials also fast asleep,
No money at the gate.
The game seems 'up to potty' now,
As they find out too late.

Avery provided an insight into the ongoing battle that was being waged between the two codes. He referred to a rugby union match which was played at the same time as the Australasia match at the Sydney Cricket Ground. The Agricultural Ground ran alongside the cricket ground so Avery was well placed to make his comment: "By the way, to show how the game has caught on here, the crowd at the match on the next ground between the Metropolitans and the American Universities team, under the old rugby union rules, only numbers from 300 to 500. Bit of a difference to our match, eh?"

There could be no doubt which code the newspapers favoured as being the people's choice. It was a far cry from the dark days of 1908 and 1909 when the fight against union had been at its height. It also represented a significant shift in attitude by the newspapers from that of 1907 over the All-Golds tour. Then the papers had always carried references to the players being paid. Now the attitude seemed to be that players were paid, but such payments were open and above board. In the past, the rugby union leadership in Sydney had made such payments 'under the table'. The newspapers knew this and thought the attitude of rugby union hypocritical.

The tourists had raised themselves for one more monumental effort and had produced a creditable draw against the combined team. But they were asked to do it once more four days later, again against Australasia, and it was to prove a game too far. On Wednesday 13 July the two teams met again. In fairness to the tourists their minds were elsewhere as they were to leave for New Zealand for the second leg of the tour on the evening of the match. The game was won 32–15 by the Australasians.

The day before the match the tour manager Joseph Houghton had to be at his most eloquent and persuasive. The SS Maheno which was to take them to New Zealand was due to leave Sydney at noon, but the second match against Australasia was due to be played on the same afternoon. Houghton managed to persuade the shipping company to delay the sailing until after the match had been played. Had he not been successful in doing so then it would have been another four days before the tourists could sail to New Zealand. That would have meant their stay there would have been reduced from two weeks to near enough only one. Who knows just what effect that could have had on the fledgling game there?

There was one notable incident in the second Australasian game, namely when Batten attempted to turn the tables on his opposite number Opai Asher. Batten received the ball in space and set off on a run. As he saw Asher approaching he determined to give him a bit of his own medicine. As Asher came in to make the tackle, Batten leapt to hurdle over him. Sadly he was not as skilled at the technique as his counterpart and mistimed his leap. The result was a collision between Batten's knee and Asher's head. Asher came off the worst – although both players needed treatment off the field Asher had sustained a gash on his head that required stitching. When they returned to the field the reports said that Asher was not the same for the rest of the game, which was hardly surprising really.

A number of the players felt that the two New Zealand players were not up to the standard of their Australian counterparts but understood why they were selected to play. Avery wrote in his letter published in Oldham on 16 August that he and others felt: "Batten put up a very good defensive game against Asher, a player who, we all think, is simply playing on a name. The same may be said of Papakura, the Maori full-back. Both played a very bad game and showed no brilliancy whatever."

In his diary Leytham wrote about this match: "We have a lot of bother with the referee and linesmen. They keep interfering with the referee and he has a lot of dubious decisions. It makes us feel as if we could walk off the field. When we play a match we have to play 13 players, referee and two linesmen. He sent one of our men off for kicking for the ball, I was captain and asked him what it was for? He said for kicking at the man.

When the whistle blew for time we had to rush for our boat... All the sailors from the war ships [were] there to set us off, as the boat left the side at 5.30 all the sailors started cheering. Papakura and Asher two New Zealand players that came over to play against us [were] on the same boat going back to New Zealand."

Avery in his letter home to the *Oldham Chronicle* was critical of the tourists' efforts in this second encounter. He wrote: "...Curzon sent off, the referee saw him kicking an opponent. Australasia were the better side and deserved to win. England defence which had been excellent all the tour was poor, head high tackles being the order. Only Thomas and Riley in the backs and Jukes and Winstanley in the forwards played well, the rest were poor."

So the first part of the tour came to a close. A feeling of bias by the referees, then as now, was noted by the players. In most matches the tourists had ended up playing with less than a full complement: if

94

injury had not robbed them of a player, then the referee had by sending someone from the field for an early bath. The reports by both Leytham and Avery show the difficulties encountered with the Australian referees' interpretation of the rules. That said, the Ashes had been decisively won.

As the tourists set sail for New Zealand they must have felt that the difficult part of the tour was over. They had come with the aim of retaining the Ashes and had achieved that. On the whole the results had been as expected. The first two games which were lost were due to a lack of conditioning from being at sea for six weeks.

For Houghton and Clifford all that mattered was that the tour outlay had been covered by the gate receipts and they were into a healthy profit. Now they were travelling to New Zealand where the standard of play would not be as demanding as in Australia. For the players it was to be a new country and new experience.

Writing in the 1930s Lomas said that "I never played better than I did when in Australia. We had a splendid time but [it was] a bit rough." He continued "It was a great experience and also educating. I believe... they [the Australians] wanted to teach us the game the way they played, we went out to do them. I think we [taught] them a lesson they are not likely to forget."

Sadly, some bad news was relayed to the tourists in general and one player in particular as they set sail for New Zealand. The *Oldham Chronicle* on 13 July made a note of it: "A sad piece of news has had to be cabled today to Batten, the Hunslet wing threequarter, who is a member of the touring team. His father has just died at his home in Hemsworth, Yorkshire. Mr Joseph Platt has sent the news to the player."

It must have been a shock to Batten who had left all his family fit and well when he had embarked on tour. There was nothing he could do except cable home his feelings to his family – he was on the other side of the world and not due back home until the middle of September, eight weeks or so in the future.

There was, however, some better news for another player as the tourists made for New Zealand. Tom Helm, the Oldham forward, had begun training again after sitting out the whole of the tour to Australia. He and the trainer felt that his knee was sufficiently recovered to start training with a view to playing in New Zealand.

The Northern Union Cup, which was presented to the
New Zealand Rugby League by the tourists.
(Courtesy Don Hammond, NZRL Museum)

7. The land of the long white cloud

The team had checked out of its headquarters, the Grand Hotel in Waverley. At the end of the second encounter with the Australasian team there was no time for entertainment following the game. Bags needed to be packed, kit bags checked and packed, and everything loaded onto the wagon to be taken down to the docks at Sydney. Immediately after the match the players left the ground still in their playing kit and boarded the SS Maheno, bound for Auckland.

Both management and players would have felt that the four or so days on the sea journey across the Tasman Sea was just the tonic they needed to refresh mind and body. However, there would have been sadness and sympathy towards Batten for the loss of his father.

The players were, of course, heading for a different country to that which they had just left. New Zealand was a far different proposition to Australia, both on and off the pitch. New Zealand had only been granted Dominion status by Great Britain in 1907. Australia had been granted this in 1901.

The tourists found that transport in the country was not as advanced as in Australia. The rail link from Wellington in the south of the island to Auckland in the north was still in its infancy. And train travel was far from comfortable.

Travel from North Island to South Island was by boat and often uncomfortable – it was at times downright dangerous. The country's economy was based around extracting gold, timber and coal from the land and agriculture was very important. Most of what was produced was bought by Britain, so the links between the two countries was very strong. The tourists did, however, find a sense of resentment among the inhabitants – they insisted they were New Zealanders and not simply an extension of Australia as some might think.

In the sporting sense they were beginning to establish their own identity and at the forefront of that was rugby union. The NZRFU was firmly behind the English RFU and would have felt threatened by the success of the All-Gold tour in 1907. They would have seen the Northern Union tour and its players as a threat to their grip on rugby in the country.

The tourists arrived in a country which was quite well developed in the population centres such as Auckland, but that quickly gave way to a rural society which was much like Britain 50 years earlier. They did, however, find the weather and the temperature much more to their liking and the lush surroundings would have reminded them of home.

Leytham was looking forward to the journey: "We passed our time in playing games on board. The distance from Sydney to Auckland is 1,281 miles. We had a good journey. We arrived at Auckland on July 17th at 2 o'clock. There was a good crowd to meet us, we had a drive round the town and then a walk round a park and council chambers, it was very fine. We are staying at the Waitemata Hotel and it is a good place. We had a reception by the Mayor of Auckland at the council chambers."

The tourists' reputation for skilful football and rough play had gone ahead of them into the New Zealand press. Also following them was the spectre of professionalism, a sensitive issue in New Zealand at the time.

Just five days after leaving Sydney they were being officially welcomed to the colony by the Mayor of Auckland L.J. Bagnall along with the president of the New Zealand League D.W. McLean. The *Auckland Evening Post* covered the event the following day, 18 July:

British footballers in Auckland

Not professional

"The Northern Union British team of footballers were welcomed by the Mayor of Auckland this morning. Mr Bagnall said he hoped the game would be played in the best spirit, free from the roughness and objectionable practices unfortunately creeping into football lately. The game ought to be played to afford enjoyment for all. The managers of the team (Messrs Houghton and Clifford) responded.

Interviewed, Mr Houghton said the team was surprised at the hold the Northern Union game had on the public in Australia. The team was fully representative of England, and had been sent as a missionary enterprise. The English [Northern] Union was prepared to lose a thousand pounds on the tour, but the receipts exceeded the most 'sanguine' expectations. The team was not composed of professionals; every man worked for a living. They were allowed 10s on board steamer, and a pound a week while playing. Each married man was allowed an additional pound while he was absent. Of any profit from the tour the players divided one third as a bonus. The allegations of rough play were exaggerated. Any unfair or objectionable tactics were severely dealt with. The team will play its first match on Wednesday against Maori."

On the subject of professionalism, at that time rugby union in New Zealand did provide payment in kind, paying for an injured player to be seen by the medical profession. Providing financial support while a player was off work was another example of the support offered to players. They claimed this was not professionalism, saying that all the players held down jobs. It would seem Houghton was keen to let the New Zealand public know that his players were not that different, they also had jobs at home.

Even at this late stage with the first game only two days away fixtures in New Zealand appear not to have been firmed up. While the tourists were still in Australia, the *Evening Post* said on 6 July: "At a meeting of the New Zealand Rugby League, held this evening, the following programme for the visit of the British team of Northern Union players to New Zealand was announced :

July 20 – Versus New Zealand Maori team in Auckland.

July 23 – Versus Auckland, at Auckland.

July 30 – Versus New Zealand, at Auckland.

The dates of the Southern matches are being arranged."

All this changed once the tourists had arrived and settled into their hotel in Auckland. The next day, following their reception at the town hall the local paper published a short statement that said: "The British Northern Union footballers will not make a southern tour. No matches will be played outside Auckland. The team will return to Sydney on 1 August."

It was widely believed that the tourists would play matches in both islands while on tour. Injuries and illness to players ensured they did not. It does appear that having made the decision that a visit to South Island was not possible, the game's leadership quickly scheduled another match, this time at Rotorua against a local team, making it a four-match tour. It was a controversy which would not go away – people were not happy about the decision, particularly those involved in the game in the South Island.

As will be seen later it would appear that the original plan had been to form a team made up of those not selected for the test match who would travel to the South Island and play a game on the same Saturday, but this never happened. Yet even as the tour was beginning, people in Nelson, Dunedin and Invercargill were hoping that they would host a match against the tourists. The *Evening Post* again reported on the discontent in the South: "The telegram from Auckland conveying the intelligence that the Englishmen would not be touring south was received with very 'mixed' feelings in Northern Union circles in the South Island. Games were expected at Nelson [and] Dunedin, while Invercargill also thought it had a chance of a visit from the English 'missionaries' who would show rugby followers and others which was the immensely superior game. Secretary Carson, says, a South lands wire has telegraphed the New Zealand League protesting against the dropping of the Southern tour and it is hoped that the protest will bear fruit."

The NU's supporters saw the tour as a chance to show the rugby spectators in the south of New Zealand how superior Northern Union rugby was to the old game. The premier rugby writer for the *Evening Post*, 'Dropkick', in a piece written on 16 April, succinctly summed up the feelings of rugby union officials in New Zealand: "The football season of 1910 opens very quietly. There is nothing sensational in the way of visits, so far as amateur football is concerned. The approaching tour of Australasia by a Northern Union professional team is not a national event, though many people will be interested perhaps to see the Northern Union played by its best exponents. Ideas may be gained as to the possibility of further improving the old game. There is no question that the approaching visit is a bold bid to establish Northern Union football on a firm basis in New Zealand. Its effects will be watched very carefully by all concerned in the welfare of rugby."

Probably the NU did not see the tour in that light, but as a profit making operation, if it helped the game down under to develop then that was a bonus. As Houghton was to say they were on "missionary work". To the hard-pressed New Zealand League officials the tour was far more important than that. It was in their eyes going to provide the very lifeblood needed for their survival.

Interestingly, 'Dropkick' was singing from a totally different hymn sheet once it became clear that no visit was to be made to the south of the country. On 23 July he wrote a piece which was scathing of the decision on the day the tourists played Auckland. His feelings were very clear: "All footballers keen about the finer shades of the game, about its possibilities of improvement and its recent developments under Northern Union rules must regret the English team is not to pursue its tour southward of Auckland. It does not say much for the missionary spirit supposed to pervade the visitors from Lancashire and Yorkshire. Methinks after all it is that comfortable couple of thousand and the danger of losing it in evangelising New Zealand to the other game that deters the bellicose gentlemen of the Northern League from

100

further extending their tour. So we shall not meet and we shall miss 'em. It is their chance, and footballers including the Union management, were quite willing to give them a fair show. However, the Englishmen are back to Sydney for more gates and gonce."

However, it had been a short but very intense tour and injuries were inevitable. By the time the team got to New Zealand they were just that, a squad able to put 13 players on the field, but unable to put a second team out. 'Dropkick' suggests that the rugby union officials were willing to give them a fair show. This would suggest that on the South Island there was a possibility of some compromise between league and union. Given the depth of feeling towards the league game by rugby union, both from their officials and the union writers, that is a little hard to believe.

However, just two days after their welcome to Auckland, the tourists got down to the job they had come to do. They were to show the people just how good they were at the new Northern Union rugby, and how entertaining the game was as well. People in New Zealand had had little chance to see that until now. The All-Gold tourists had returned home two years earlier to find they had no clubs or competition in which to participate. Baskerville's death and its effect can be seen here. Many New Zealand players who would have preferred to stay at home and strengthen the game there, signed for Australian clubs or joined Northern Union clubs in England. It is hard to imagine that Baskerville would have sat back and done nothing in this situation. Rugby union had not only banned the All-Gold tourists for life, but also barred them from being allowed to enter any rugby ground in the country under their control.

They did the same thing later, in 1908, when a little known group of tourists returned home from Australia. As the All-Gold tourists were leaving Australia for home, a party consisting of Maori were about to start a tour to Australia. When they left New Zealand they were under the belief that they were undertaking a rugby union tour. When they arrived at the docks in Sydney the party that greeted them was the New South Wales Rugby League. It was explained that they were the party who had in fact issued the invitation. A hastily organised meeting was held and the players agreed that they would play the Northern Union brand of rugby.

That is the popular belief, although sadly the truth may be a little different, certainly Asher was well aware of which code he was taking his tour party to play. He gave an interview to a reporter just prior to leaving for Sydney on Monday 25 May. It appeared in the *Evening Post* on Friday 29 May as the tourists were about to land in Sydney: "As reported by telegram the professional Maori football team under the guidance of Mr Albert Asher (manager) left Auckland on Monday night in the Moana for Sydney. In conversation with Mr Asher just prior to the steamer's departure, a *Herald* representative was told that the combination had taken some getting together... The New South Wales professional league had invited them over, and were making the financial arrangements for the trip which would be carried out under their guidance."

It is not clear, however, if every member of the tour party was aware of the fact they were to play Northern Union or Rugby Union once on Australian soil. Just three days later the same newspaper in Wellington printed the following item: "The Maori footballers will play the Northern Union game during their tour in New South Wales, after witnessing a couple of matches and themselves practising the new style of rugby the team took a vote of their members which favoured the new in place of the old rugby."

Perhaps their decision had been influenced by the fact the league had taken all the Maori tourists to watch a club game. Having seen the Northern Union in action they were keen to play it. Their captain Opai Asher said to the press that they would master the new rules after a day of practice. The story of the tour party switching from union to league is probably a myth. It may have been dreamt up by Giltinan as a way of getting at the rugby union officials.

Sadly the tour was cut short after legal wrangling off the pitch and disagreements with James Giltinan. In October 1907, Asher had entered into a verbal agreement with an Australian called Robert Jack to organise a tour which would take place in 1908. The two could not reach an agreement and Asher then approached the New South Wales Rugby League and Giltinan. Once the tour was under way Jack claimed he was entitled to 5 per cent of the gate money for the tour matches. Asher obviously disagreed because there was no contract, however the courts agreed with Jack. Asher then argued with Giltinan over the gate receipts at certain matches and the split between the two became so great that the two could not reconcile their differences. The Maori returned home well before they had planned. On their return the New Zealand Rugby Union promptly banned them all for life, claiming that they were all professionals and thus could not play rugby union again.

Ironically, rather than damaging the Northern Union game in the colony, it strengthened it. It made available a large number of top-quality Maori players.

Opai was actually the name of a famous race horse that had won many steeplechases in New Zealand. As Asher began to use his hurdling technique more often, so the name was applied to him. Asher, and players like him, when added to the returning All-Gold players, gave the New Zealand Rugby League a nucleus of top-quality players around which to build club sides in the Auckland area.

Most of the players from that All-Gold tour had either retired from the game, or had returned to Britain to ply their new trade. Johnson and Todd had gone to Wigan, 'Jum' Turtill had signed for St Helens. And, with great irony, as the tourists were landing in New Zealand, Bill 'Massa' Johnson and Charlie Seeling were leaving those shores to go and play in England. Others had crossed the Tasman Sea to play for Australian clubs, although the three countries would later agree a transfer embargo to stop such movements of players. The New Zealand public were keen to see Northern Union rugby played by the top players, and they were not disappointed with the action they saw.

The tourists awoke on Wednesday 20 July to be greeted by torrential rain. The rain continued unabated all morning and as they made their way out to the ground they found the playing surface almost submerged in water. Around 5,000 brave souls turned out to watch them take on the New Zealand Maori team in the Northern Union's first ever game in New Zealand. The press was pleased with their endeavours as the match report shows:

Northern Union game
Maori easily beaten by British team
"The first match of the British Northern Union rugby football team was played here today against the New Zealand Maori team in drenching rain and a ground that was practically under water. The showing of the Englishmen under these adverse conditions was so good that further matches are being eagerly anticipated. The attendance today was over 5,000. The Maori kicked off, and the ball, after an exchange of kicks went out into touch at half-way, and from a scrum the Maori secured, but the English forwards were too fast, and play was stopped about the Maori 25, where a free-kick was taken by Lomas. A good attempt at goal failed. From the kick-off all the English backs tried some passing, but the ball was too slippery to hold, and the Maori got relief by a good dribbling rush. Lomas made two good attempts at

goal, and then, from out of a pretty passing rush Riley received, and ended up a fine run by scoring the Britishers first points in New Zealand. Lomas made a good attempt at goal, but failed. Britain 3 Maori 0.

From the drop-out the Englishmen came back to the attack and their line of backs gave promise of what they could do with a dry ball on a fine ground. A loose rush saw Bert Jenkins secure and... he touched down behind the posts. Lomas converted. Britain 8 Maori 0.

From the kick-off the Maori attacked for a while, but the Britishers were soon back, and a pretty piece of passing saw Smith score under the posts. Lomas converted. Britain 13 Maori 0

A spell of more even play followed. The Maori forwards attacked but the rush was resultless and play worked up to their quarters again, where the Britishers were given a free kick. Lomas kicked a goal... British 15 Maori 0.

The rain had stopped and the sun was shining when play resumed. From a scrum at the centre Smith secured and sent to Davies from whom it travelled to Lomas and on to B. Jenkins who scored. Lomas failed with the kick. Britain 18 Maori 0.

The ball was hardly in play again when an Englishman started a passing rush, which ended in B. Jenkins scoring. Lomas failed at goal. Britain 21 Maori 0.

The Maori forwards worked into their visitors' territory, but their backs gave them no support and play was soon into Maori quarters again, where a free-kick was given against them and Lomas found the posts. The spell ended with the score Britain 23 Maori 0.

No spell was taken, the players changing over and recommencing straight away. The British backs secured almost at once, and a good passing rush was concluded by B. Jenkins cleverly cutting in and scoring a try, which Leytham failed to convert. Britain 26 Maori 0.

When play resumed the Maori brightened up, and for a time had the best of matters. In a tackle Rouwhiriwhiri was hurt and play was suspended for some time. From his own 25 Lomas secured and dashing through the pack scored. He took the kick at goal and failed and the game ended shortly after with the scores Britain 29 Maori 0."

It was obviously not a day for goalkickers, but Wigan centre Bert Jenkins must have created an impression with his four tries. The reporter hinted at just how good the tourists would be on a dry ground, and the game whetted the appetite of the paying public for their next outing at the weekend, against a side representing Auckland. The match had not proved to be much of a test for the tourists and perhaps the old adage 'the weather is a great leveller' was true in this case.

Even the tourists were far from happy as Leytham recalled in his diary: "Played the Maori on 20 July, had our photo taken with our straw hats on. Then we got ready for the match. It rained very hard, the field was flooded. The game started at 3 o'clock, we soon got to scoring Bert Jenkins 4 tries, Riley 1, Lomas 1, Smith I and Lomas 3 goals. It was not a good match we could not stick to the ball, it was all kick and rush. We were invited to a smoker by the League Committee at the Ferate Club and enjoyed a good evening.

The day after July 21 we were invited by Mr Todd, father of Lance Todd who plays for Wigan. We drove through the Park and visited at stud and then drove to his home to Otahulu and had a good dinner. We had a good concert and were all made heartily welcome."

Leytham's diary shows the welcome and hospitality the players were given in New Zealand As he continued after the visit to Lance Todd's father: "It was raining going and coming back... it didn't forget to come down. It is a very fine country, we had about a 30-mile drive over country to get back to our hotel. After dinner we were invited to go over to the island called Davenport. We went to the house of a Wigan man, there was myself, Sharrock and four Wigan men. One of their wives made a good potato pie and it was the best we have had since we came out here. So we had a good chat and a splendid evening. The day after was wet, after dinner we went with George Dell for a motor drive, we covered 30 miles over country and it did rain but we was alright. At night we were invited with William Wynyard to his house for dinner and then went to his father's for supper and enjoyed ourselves very well. We got back to our hotel about 12 o'clock...

July 23rd at 7.15 in the morning came a knock at the bedroom door I jumped up to open it and there stood Perkins from Torresholme, I was surprised. He told me his wife and sister was down stairs so I went down to see them and they were doing alright. So they went across to Davenport to see his sister, they all came back to watch the match. We kicked off at 3 o'clock and were greeted with cheers, it was a one sided game and we won 52 points to 9."

It does seem that the atmosphere was more relaxed and friendly in New Zealand than it had been in Sydney. During the week the tourists organised a training session and played a game among themselves.

The intention was to give Tom Helm a run out to test his knee. Writing home on 23 July, Bert Avery said: "I am sorry to say that Tom Helm's knee did not stand the test last Monday and that he won't be able to play at all on the tour. The doctor says that he has fluid on the knee and nothing but rest will cure it, so Tom has to rest." So Helm's ill-fated tour and hopes of playing came to an end.

Saturday dawned and it was still raining. As the tourists made their way to Victoria Park at Freeman's Bay where the match was being played, they would have been pleased to see that the weather was not stopping the New Zealand public from turning out to watch the match against Auckland. Around 10,000 fans turned up to see a display of power and pace which gave their opponents no respite and must have impressed all those present. The *Auckland Evening Post* had a match report on Monday 25 July:

Northern League game

Auckland badly beaten

The British team played their second match of the tour at Victoria Park this afternoon, when they met the Auckland representatives. The weather was showery and there was a large attendance. There was an absence of sun and wind.

The Englishmen won the toss. Jackson kicked off for Auckland from the western end. Auckland were the first to attack, and [after] the forwards [took] charge Jackson made a fine opening and sent to Seagar, who, with a fast dash scored. Jackson failed at goal.

The game was very fast, travelling up and down at a great pace. From a sensational passing run, Jenkins broke through, and scored. Lomas converted.

England's game was very fast and open. Auckland attacked for a space, but the Englishmen eventually got going. A loose dribbling rush ended in Jukes falling on the ball. Lomas goaled.

Auckland rallied, and the Englishmen forced. England were giving a good display and Auckland were continually on the defence. Davies set his backs going and Avery scored the third try. Lomas was again successful with the kick.

The next try came immediately afterwards, through the agency of Riley. Lomas failed to kick the goal.

Auckland made a dash, but it was only a temporary rally. The visitors attacked again, Leytham adding a try. He goaled. England 23 Auckland 3.

The game was very fast and exciting. England's passing was wonderful. Tries were added by Riley (2), Jukes and Kershaw, three of which were converted by Lomas. At half-time the score was: England 41 Auckland 3.

Second half: The visitors were immediately on the attack from the kick-off, but Auckland cleared, and set up a hot attack. The visitors defence was severely tested, but was solid, and they had no difficulty in repulsing the invasion. Auckland were making a much better showing than in the first spell. The pace, however, was being maintained, the Auckland forwards in particular putting dash into their work. Jenkins, the full-back for England, worked brilliantly, saving his side time after time. Eventually the Auckland attack proved successful. Smith, making a fine opening, sent to Asher, and the latter shook off Riley and Jenkins, and scored amidst applause. Jackson failed with the kick. England 41 Auckland 6.

Auckland now put a lot of heart into their work, but the visitors retaliated, coming away with a brilliant dash, and Lomas dribbled over and scored. Rich failed with the kick.

The locals were more than holding their own with the Englishmen, but [their] play lacked finish, and hard tackling nullified the efforts of both sides... Then Nolan put Auckland on the attack by a tricky feinting run, but England retaliated and Winstanley scored. Lomas converted. Auckland were soon defending again, and Leytham scored near the corner. The kick failed. Auckland made a final rally and Griffin scored. The kick was resultless, and the game ended. England 52 Auckland 9.

The attendance was estimated at 10,000. A light rain fell in the early part of the game, but the weather cleared up shortly after play commenced. The game was fast and exciting throughout, an altogether brilliant exhibition."

Other reports also recognised the great performance by the NU side, but felt that they eased up in the second half. If this was so it might have been to ensure the local players were not completely demoralised. Clearly the tourists were creating a favourable impression on both the supporters and the reporters covering the games. The Northern Union style of rugby was so much faster, the tackling more forceful and the action on the field seemingly more non-stop than the rugby they were used to seeing. The New Zealand League officials must have been delighted. Their union counterparts on the other hand must have been worried because, in spite of all their efforts, this professional game simply would not go away.

It must be remembered that almost all the reporters watching the tourists play had probably never seen Northern Union rugby played by top class players. As a result they had only top-class rugby union players to compare the tourists with. When Avery sent his letter back to Oldham following the Auckland match, he attached an article commenting on the game by the *Auckland Star*. It makes interesting reading even after 100 years. Of the tourists he wrote: "As a team they are a remarkably short, thick set, heavy lot of men, but they are remarkably fast – much faster than our men and they can play the game hard from starting whistle to the no-side bell...

"The English Northern Union player is a totally different kind of footballer... from the English Rugby Union player. He is much superior physically, he can stay out a game better and keep up his end better if things happen to be strenuous This last team, which plays the reformed Rugby, would make the very best New Zealand amateur team ever picked put its very best foot forward to win. Our greatest 'All-Black' teams never had a set of forwards who could out-run, out-weight and outwit this side, and their best and liveliest backs could never have shown these men anything to speak of in the matter of accurate passing, fast running, straight and strong kicking and safe tackling..."

He went on to extol the virtues of the tourists' tackling and the manner in which they controlled the opposition in the tackle. He considered the performance of Chic Jenkins at full-back against Auckland to be "one of the finest ever seen in that position in Auckland either amateur or professionally. His fielding and kicking were magnificent throughout." No wonder that the rugby union officials were so worried.

The NU tourists could not, however, rest on their laurels, for the New Zealand rugby league had arranged the fixture against Rotorua, in the Bay of Plenty area. On Monday the team boarded the local express train out to the Bay of Plenty in preparation for the game on Wednesday. Rotorua is a beautiful tourist spot and then, as now, was famous for its health-giving thermal springs. Given the sulphurous fumes that the springs gave off which pervaded the air, the tourists would have felt at home – at least those from the Widnes area, where the local club were not known as the Chemics for nothing. The smell that came from the chemical works in the town was not too different from the one they experienced in Rotorua.

For Leytham and the rest of the party the hospitality seems to have continued: "We went for a walk around with Mr Puckett and then went for my tea to his house. We left Auckland on Monday July 24 at 10 o'clock and arrived Rotorua at 6.30 at night and had a good dinner that we were invited to by the committee. The night before leaving we were all received by the Maori chiefs and had a good time. We left Rotorua on July 29 ready for our next match with New Zealand."

Sadly there are very few records of the match in the local press. Original copies of the newspapers of the time, such as the *Bay of Plenty Times*, seem to have been destroyed by fire some years ago. Perhaps it was not considered an important match because the week was to see the run up to the test match against New Zealand. None of the various regional newspapers of the time carried any mention of the Rotorua game. The local newspaper of the time for Rotorua was *The Hot Lakes Chronicle* and there is no known copy of the paper in New Zealand. Fortunately, the Alexander Turnbull Library in New Zealand has references to the match from *The New Zealand Herald* on 27 and 29 July. The only other record to date of anything regarding this game comes from a 1933 *Rugby League Annual*, published in New Zealand. That gives only the bare information of the Rotorua team and nothing else. The team was stated to be:

Tiki Papakura, Fernandez, F. Woodward, Reke, Harp, N. McRae, (replaced by Lane), R. Hastedt, Davidson, Rogers, Crowther, Ngapapa, Childs, McCallum.

The reference made to the game in the *New Zealand Herald* on 27 July was on the day of the match so while confirming that it actually took place there is no report on the action on the field. It read: "The team on their arrival here last evening were officially received by the league representatives. The weather promises to be fair for the entertainment of the team, for which the Government has provided a very ample and effective scheme. Today they visited Waimanga, where the great outbreak of thermal activity occurred. The round trip occupied the whole day. In the evening a grand ball and euchre party was held. [Euchre was a popular card game in New Zealand at this time] The dinner tendered at the Lake House Hotel, on the shores of Ohinemuto, where the team are quartered was a convivial reunion of sportsmen... The welcome was thoroughly characteristic and hearty."

There was also a small article which referred to the Challenge Cup that the Northern Union was to present to the newly formed New Zealand Rugby League. It was not known for sure whether the cup was made in England and transported down under or commissioned in

New Zealand. However, given that the maker's name on the trophy was Fattorini of Bradford and they had made the Rugby League Challenge Cup it is reasonable to assume that the cup was made in Bradford and shipped out with the tour party. Once in New Zealand the cup was presented to the New Zealand Rugby League. Interestingly, the Northern Union was prepared to transport a cup for the New Zealand Rugby League but not for the Australians. Maybe this was because of Houghton's very strong connection with the founding of the NZRL.

The article also highlighted the hospitality extended to the visitors. It said: "The handsome Challenge Cup presented to the New Zealand Football League by the Northern Union is now on view in Mr J.S. Dickson's window, Queens Street. It is of solid silver, of beautiful design and it bears the arms of England and New Zealand enamelled. The cup stands about 18 [inches] high.

"Mr Hugh J. Ward, who is an enthusiastic admirer of football, has taken a lively interest in the British team now touring in this province. After last Saturday's match at Victoria Park Mr Ward generously extended an invitation to the British team to attend a special football evening at His Majesty's Theatre on Friday night, when they return from Rotorua. The invitation has since been cordially accepted and the managers of the Auckland Northern Union League have especially thanked Mr Ward for the highly appreciated assistance this is rendering the league in providing entertainment for the visiting footballers. The whole of the British representatives will be present on Friday night to witness the performance of *The Fencing Master* as the guests of the popular actor-manager."

The cup is now known as The Rugby League Cup and was first contested for in 1911 when Auckland defeated Wellington in a challenge match for the cup. Auckland were not to lose the trophy until 1921 when South Auckland, now known as Waikato, won it. Since that time the cup has been won by almost every province in New Zealand.

In the match, the tourists, as expected, ran out comfortable winners 54–18. It was yet another big score and sounded ominous warnings to the New Zealand side and the press. The tourists were back at their very best and ready for the game which they believed would be their last on the tour.

While the tourists were in Rotorua, the New Zealand Rugby League Council was meeting and a number of issues were discussed and recorded in the minutes: "At the ninth meeting of the Council on 27 July 1910, the president stated that the managers of the British team regretted being unable to extend this tour to Taranaki, Nelson and Southland. The secretary reported that the Silver Cup (Northern Union Cup) presented by the visitors on behalf of the parent body had been placed in sake keeping. The appointment of Mr Sharrock in the England New Zealand match was cancelled in favour of Mr J. Stanaway."

The Stanaway referred to, who was to referee the first ever test in New Zealand between the two teams was Jack Stanaway who was in fact a Maori called Hone Haira. Many Maori at this time also used European names. He was a former tourist, having toured Australia back in 1908 with Opai Asher's team. The reason for the change of referee is clear from the Council minutes: "Mr Sharrock was also suspended for offensive remarks made at the meeting".

As the Saturday morning dawned all would have been glad to see the sun coming up into a clear blue sky. There was a light breeze as the NU team clambered aboard the wagons that would take them out to the Domain Cricket Ground, the venue for the test match. As the team approached the ground they would have been pleased when they saw a large crowd following them to the ground. It seemed that Northern Union rugby was proving to be as big an attraction in New Zealand as it had proved to be in Australia. The game lived up to all expectations of the tourists' performance, as the match report shows. It was published in the *Evening Post* on 1 August:

England put up a big score

A huge attendance

The match... was played on the Domain Ground this afternoon. New Zealand played with a strong sun and light breeze behind them. After a short series of exchanges, Seager made a fine opening, and New Zealand attacked first, and continued on the offensive until England forced. After a spell of lively play between the half-way and the English line, Batten opened up cleverly, and set his whole team moving in a passing rush. Jenkins crossed the line and grounded the ball, but was called back for a throw forward. England continued to attack and eventually Smith got possession, sent to Thomas to Leytham, who scored after a good run at the corner. Lomas failed with the kick at goal. England 3 New Zealand 0.

New Zealand rallied on resuming and a free-kick allowed Jackson to register a beautiful goal. England 3 New Zealand 2.

New Zealand forwards were holding their own and the visitors were not displaying the brilliancy of last week. Eventually England were awarded a free-kick, and Lomas kicked a goal. England 5 New Zealand 2. New Zealand caused some excitement by setting up a lively attack. Buckland scored and Asher failed to goal. England 5 New Zealand 5.

Encouraged by the success, New Zealand again attacked and McDonald scored. New Zealand 10 England 5. The game was now very fast, and the home team was showing surprisingly good form. Leytham got away but [Ernie] Asher caught him from behind and the chance was lost England kept up the attack, and Avery scored, Lomas converting. England 10 New Zealand 10.

The New Zealand forwards were holding their own, and counteracting the work of the English backs. After both sides had taken part in an exciting attack Seager scored. New Zealand 15 England 10.

On resuming New Zealand made things lively, but from his own 25 Jenkins broke away, and looked like scoring. Chorley averted the danger with a splendid tackle. The New Zealand forwards relieved the pressure with a fast forward rush, but the strong running Englishmen brought the leather back to the line and Sharrock, picking up smartly, potted a beautiful goal. New Zealand 15 England 12.

The New Zealand forwards rushed the ball to England's 25, but their play was faulty and England returned the attack, Chorley and E. Asher saving cleverly. England were not to be denied. Mason starting a passing run, Smith got over. Lomas failed with the kick. England 15 New Zealand 15.

England came back to the attack and were now showing all their true form. The game was fairly even until gradually the New Zealand defence was beaten down. Kershaw with a clever bit of work, scored. Lomas failed at goal. England 18 New Zealand 15. This was the turning point in the game. England quickly added to their scores, the tries being secured by Leytham and B. Jenkins (2) in quick succession, one of which was converted and the score read: England 29 New Zealand 15. New Zealand were making a plucky but ineffectual fight, and after another brilliant passing run, Lomas scored and converted. England 34 New Zealand 15.

The next score came from a forward scramble, Avery being the try-getter. Lomas converted. A second afterwards, another fast run ended in Thomas scoring, Lomas again converting. England 44 New Zealand 15. Shortly after, from another spectacular run, Avery scored. Lomas failed with the kick. New Zealand made a final rally, and after a lot of loose forward play, Hughes scored and Jackson converted. England 44 New Zealand 20.

Only a few minutes remained to play but it was sufficient time to enable Kershaw to score. Thomas converted, and the bell rang with the scores: England 52 New Zealand 20

It was estimated the attendance was fifteen to seventeen thousand. The game was another bright exhibition, and the interest was maintained to the end."

When the tourists took the field in this match little did they know that one of the opposition was a mystery. In the New Zealand pack was a forward listed simply as Fred Jackson. Jackson kicked two goals in the match, which is unremarkable. What was remarkable was that he had been on tour in New Zealand in 1908 with the British Lions rugby union squad. He was suspended and sent home for being a professional, this after being one of the foremost rugby union forwards in England prior to his Lions selection. The allegation was that he had signed as a professional for Swinton back in 1902. What was more mysterious was that Jackson was not his real name, and he never revealed to his family what his real identity was.

The other player the tourists would have known was the New Zealand full-back Alf Chorley. He was born in Westmoreland in England in 1874, and played rugby union for Halifax prior to the 1895 split. He also played in the NU for Swinton, and emigrated to New Zealand in 1908. He played for Ponsonby and Auckland.

In what was probably his last letter home, Avery wrote about the game. Once again, it seems the injury jinx struck with Batten having to leave the field and Kershaw was taken out of the pack to fill the void on the wing. In an interview with the one of the Auckland Rugby League officials, Barry Brigham, Avery sheds light on just what was to happen to the home union's share of the test gate: "Mr Brigham informed me that with the money they had made out of our match here they are going on a mission throughout New Zealand to try and make converts to the Northern Union game. Taranaki, Wellington, Nelson, Canterbury, Otago and Hawkes Bay are places they intend playing at on their mission. Everything seems clear for them as the teams named have written for the Auckland team to visit them, from which one gathers that the days of the Rugby Union here are numbered."

Part of the crowd for the New Zealand versus England test match
at Auckland on 30 July 1910. (Courtesy Don Hammond, NZRL Museum)

The 1910 New Zealand rugby league team.
(Courtesy Don Hammond, NZRL Museum)

The tourists enjoying a boat trip in New Zealand. (Courtesy Rob Deller)

Visiting a geyser in New Zealand. (Courtesy Rob Deller)

True to his word, Auckland did sent a team to tour in the south of the country. Later in 1910 an Auckland team went on tour playing games in the deep south of the country, at Dunedin in Otago, Invercargill and Bluff in Southlands. They bypassed Christchurch but did stop off to play a final match in Nelson. Thus the tourists' visit did bring some benefit for the new code as a whole in New Zealand.

After the test match Leytham records that the hospitality continued: "The next day after the match I went out for the day to Mr Puckett's house. We watched a military funeral and we were asked to go to Church at night. There were only about 8 there. The parson preached about us and prayed that we should have a pleasant voyage home. The day after 1 August we were packing up as we had to be on the boat at 5 o'clock but did not go out till 10.30. There was a large crowd seeing us off, when the boat was leaving the stage they gave us the war cry and we gave them a cheer."

So the short visit to New Zealand was at an end. Surely no one involved could have dreamed just how successful it had been. Northern Union rugby had been firmly entrenched in the minds of even the most ardent rugby union followers there. The tourists had played brilliant rugby at times, shown just how much faster their game was and how much stronger they tackled. The two managers must have been delighted with the outcome of the short stay in New Zealand. As the party was about to embark again onto the Maheno for the return journey to Sydney, Mr Houghton gave a last interview to the *Auckland Evening Post:* "Mr J.H. Houghton... said he had received a cabled invitation to play a match against a team in Sydney on Saturday next, and he had replied accepting the invitation. He did not know whether it was against an Australian or New South Wales League team. The portion of the party not playing in that match will leave Sydney by the Orient liner Otranto, which leaves Sydney for London prior to the match. Those taking part will journey overland by train to Melbourne where they will rejoin their party.

"When asked whether he would give particulars of the New Zealand takings, Mr Houghton said they had nothing to hide. The New Zealand takings amounted to £875/8s made up as follows: Match v New Zealand Maori at Victoria Park £73/8s; against Auckland representatives at Victoria Park £323/8s; against Rotorua representatives at Rotorua £45/3s; and against New Zealand representatives at the Domain, £433/9s.

The amount was divided in the proportion of 60 per cent to the British team, who had to pay all their own expenses, such as fares and hotel bills, and 40 per cent to the New Zealand Rugby League who had to stand the expense of ground fees, advertising and local expenses. It would be seen that they would lose money by the New Zealand tour, but they did not mind that. Theirs was a missionary visit, and they had not expected to make money.

"Asked why they had not sent a team south, Mr. Houghton said they had been unable to do so for several good reasons. One was the limited time, and another that the team had been reduced in strength by illness and accident. He had proposed to send a team south to play a match simultaneously with that against the New Zealand team last Saturday, but found he was unable to do so at the last minute, owing to the fact that they had not sufficient playing men available.

"Regarding future visits of teams, he and Mr Clifford would certainly advise the Northern Union on their return to keep up a series of visits between Australia and England. He could not pass an opinion as to whether the next team to tour England would be purely Australian or Australasian. That would be decided later.

"The team were given a hearty send-off, cheers being exchanged as the Maheno drew away from the wharf."

So the short tour was over, but the results and consequences of the visit would last far longer than the two weeks or so the visitors had been in the country. It was true the tour had lost money but it had achieved far more than financial rewards. It had shown many people in the country just what Northern Union rugby was all about. It had added a little to the leagues coffers and so sustained them a little longer as they fought to establish the game there. More importantly it had shown that the Northern Union would be supportive of them even though they were 12,000 miles or more away from the game's heartlands in the north of England.

It must be said, however, with the benefit of 100 years of hindsight that the tour could have done a great deal more for the game in New Zealand than it did. The New Zealand Rugby League was only formed in April 1910 and then only set up in order to liaise with the Northern Union regarding the tour. The game was to all intents and purposes only developed and entrenched in the Auckland area.

The feelings of the union officials can be seen from a report that appeared in the *Evening Post* on 15 May, well before the tourists set foot on New Zealand soil: "It was moved by Mr J. Hutchison, on behalf

117

of the Otago Union 'That it be an instruction to the committee of management to consider carefully the rules of the game, with a view to their improvement where possible'... The motion was seconded by Mr Wilford MP who expressed an opinion that within two years' time the New Zealand Rugby Union would be playing the game of the Northern Rugby Union. He meant playing it under amateur conditions. He saw it played in England five years ago and he had lately been talking with Major Davy an old rugby player who saw the Northern Union game played in Sydney last month and they both were of the opinion that the newer game was much faster and more interesting to the public than the old game was."

So apprehensive were they that, along with the New Zealand Rugby Union and the New South Wales Rugby Union, they set out to alter the rules of the game in an attempt to make it more attractive to spectators. The only way they could achieve that was, to a large extent, to adopt the Northern Union style of play. Some time later their joint application to the Rugby Union in London, to modify the rules was turned down flat.

In 1912 the Northern Union had grown so much in the Auckland area that the proposal of a tour to the area by players of that code from New South Wales, saw the Canterbury Rugby Union go into panic mode, when they discussed the threat being posed by the spread of the Northern Union code. So worried were they that there was even a proposal – sadly turned down – that they themselves adopt the rugby league rules. The argument was that at least then they would remain in control of the game.

They had good reason to be worried if the reports of that tour and the attitudes it provoked in the press are anything to go by. They simply reinforce the view that had the 1910 tour gone south it would have stimulated more development of Northern Union rugby. Much more than did the domestic tour by Auckland in 1910. 'Dropkick' writing in the *Evening Post* on 31 August 1912 of a match he witnessed played by the Australian team, was in no doubt which was the better code: "At last Wellington has seen an exhibition of the Northern Union game, and it has left many footballers thinking hard. Let it be said honestly, and at the start, that the majority of those who saw Saturday's match between New South Wales and Wellington representatives appeared pleased with the game. Nor could any unbiased spectators fail to admit that it is fast, clean and open, three qualifications all more or less the outcome of alterations and modifications in the old rugby rules."

He went on to extol the virtues of the fast open game he had seen and pointed out the failings of the old rugby game as played in the country at the time. He ended the report by laying on the line just what the rugby union authorities had to do: "...One of these fine days the rugby union will have to come into line with the league amendments to the rules. Sooner or later it must be realised that if there is anything in the league game that makes for improvement in play and added interest from the spectators' point of view it is only folly to ignore it... the best way forward for the rugby union to combat the professional game is to offer the public a game which is equally attractive."

Strong stuff from the reporter, but it must have struck home. Just a little time later, around the outbreak of the First World War, the New Zealand Rugby Union actually gave the Auckland Rugby Union permission to play what was euphemistically referred to as the 'Auckland Rules'. They did so in an attempt to fight back against the popularity of the league game in the area at the time. The decision was made to do this knowing full well that the union authorities in England would never give their approval, perhaps they were never told...

The 1912 New South Wales NU tour saw them visit Wellington and Canterbury. They also played matches at Wanganui, Tarinaki, Hawkes Bay and finally returned to Auckland.

There was one incident in the whole of that 1912 tour which was of tremendous importance and poignant if only because of its apparent insignificance. In the game against Wellington the match report in the *Evening Post* on 26 August had one sentence which stood out: "Bradley centre threequarter hurt a shoulder early and retired G. Baskiville taking his place".

There is little doubt that this was the brother of Albert Baskerville. It was probably George Baskiville, who would have been 23 years old at that time. If that was the case it must have been a very poignant moment both for the player and his family. To be playing against a touring team just four years after the death of a brother who instigated the playing of Northern Union rugby in New Zealand. There would have been a great deal of pride in the Baskiville family that afternoon and not a little sadness at the way things had turned out.

119

It would seem it was no coincidence that the following season saw club competitions launched in Canterbury and Wellington. Sadly, the First World War was to ravage the game in the country as it did in Great Britain. Northern Union club rugby was very much in its infancy. Many of the administrators of the game were also players and went off to fight in the war, unlike the rugby union clubs of whom many of the administrators were much older men, too old to be called up to fight. Those clubs were in a better position to keep going than were the league clubs.

The 1910 tour went a long way to establishing the game in New Zealand, as was shown by its subsequent development. It is also noticeable that for much of its history, the game in New Zealand was played solely on an amateur basis, showing that the players there preferred to play rugby league, rather than doing so for any financial gain. Obviously many New Zealanders played professionally in Australia and Great Britain, and made a huge contribution to the sport's international development, as has their international team, including their first World Cup triumph in 2008.

8. Homeward bound

The players and management settled down for the four-day sea voyage back to Sydney. Their plans had once again changed at short notice. They had originally believed that they were simply returning to Sydney to catch a connecting ship to England. However, as Houghton let slip in his final interview in New Zealand, the New South Wales League had telegraphed him with a request to play one final game back in Sydney. Houghton and Clifford, seeing the opportunity for one last big gate receipt and ever mindful of the tour profits, had agreed to the suggestion.

The players, as always, simply got on with the job. That seems to have been a common thread that ran through the whole of this tour. They were just happy to play, by doing so they increased the chances of the profits being larger.

Bert Avery, in a letter to the *Oldham Chronicle*, published on 5 September, while he and the others were still at sea on the way home, gave an insight into the view he and others had of the tour manager and its finances: "Now, just a word about our manager, Mr Houghton. Our players in general say that the Northern Union officials could not have selected a better man. He looks after the players just like a father and is very keen as regards the players' interests, which every player admires him for and supports him in every respect. We have made the tour very successful financially as well as by football, so that there is nothing to worry about."

The acceptance of this last game shows just how much support Joseph Houghton and John Clifford had from the players. It did, however, throw the organisation of the return trip into chaos for the managers. It was hastily arranged that the players not required for the game would leave Sydney by ship as previously arranged. The players involved in the game would not board the ship in Sydney. After it they would travel overland by train to Melbourne to board the ship there. The two managers would remain in Sydney a little longer to clear up any last-minute hitches, sort out financial arrangements and, more importantly, ensure the gate receipts were safely banked and arrangements made for these funds to be transferred to Leeds.

The players arrived in Sydney in poor spirits as Leytham noted: "We are having some bad weather between Auckland and Sydney. We are about 10 hours late, the wind is howling and rain is coming down. The boat is jumping there is a lot of the boys sick, some dare not get up. We arrived Sydney at 10.30 on August 5th. All the other players except the team that was picked to play... had to board the Otranto on August 6. The team travelled overland and [caught] them at Melbourne."

The team had just two days to recover from a very rough sea journey and the resultant sea-sickness. They also had to prepare for the last game of the tour. The Australian Northern Union supporters' final memory of the tourists would be their performance in this game.

There is an irony about the whole events surrounding the match. The tour had begun way back in May with half the tour party arriving in Sydney while awaiting the arrival of the rest of the squad. Now, in early August, once again half the team was in Sydney while the other half was on the ocean sailing home. And once again, the players chosen for the game were on their way to the Agricultural Ground to play a New South Wales side.

However, on the same day the full New South Wales team, Messenger included, were in Queensland playing the Queensland representative side. It was a measure of the drawing power of the Northern Union tourists, combined with it being the last opportunity people had to see the team play, which led to around 20,000 spectators attending this final match. The gate receipts of £630 would have been welcomed by Houghton and Clifford.

The game was not over-taxing for the tourists, the opposition second string proving no match as Leytham recalled: "We played New South Wales on August 6 and beat them by 50 points to 12. We had our own way and could score when we liked. It would have been more if we had been on land a day or two [but] we could feel the effects of the boat. We had a good crowd of about 20,000 people. I enjoyed Sunday with Mr Barnsley, his son came over to England with the Australia Cricket team. We [sailed] up the harbour and then walked round an ostrich farm, it was very warm. The next day we had a look round Sydney for the last time and had to leave the same day August 8th at 8 o'clock at night. We had a good send off. We had a good ride before us the distance is over 500 miles and arrived at Melbourne at 2.30 in the afternoon on August 9th. None of the boys came to meet us so we hired a drag to take us to the steamer. They had had a good trip to Melbourne and were settled down to the boat. We left the next day August 10th at 3 o'clock."

The team travelled home via Colombo, Egypt and the Red Sea. When they sailed past Sicily they saw a volcano erupting. The final ports of call were Marseilles and Gibraltar. They arrived back in Plymouth.

It was a pity really that Leytham was such a modest man about his playing abilities. Had he not been so, perhaps the diary may have given a greater insight into the matches on tour, and provided some idea of the strategies and tactics employed by the team. They trained twice a day generally and eased down as the match day approached. There is nothing about the Australian and New Zealand players they faced. There is also no information about how the players got on with each other and their feelings when not selected to play in the big matches.

His only insights into the playing side of the tour are when he expresses his opinions on the referees and linesmen. He seemed to be expressing the feelings of all the tourists when saying they often felt like walking off the field such was the strength of ill feeling.

Leytham was more interested in writing about the journey than he was in the rugby. Still, his words do provide a brief glimpse into the world as it was in 1910 in Australia and New Zealand.

Back in England, as the tourists were on board ship returning home, the Northern Union Committee met on 9 August 1910. The minutes record the first reference to the possibility of a number of end-of-tour matches being staged: "The secretary was instructed to open up correspondence with a view to arranging an exhibition match by our Australian touring team at Plymouth on September 17th or 19th. It was resolved that a similar match be played at Headingley, Leeds on September 19th or 21st. The gate at the last named match to be divided ½ to the 26 touring players and ½ to Bristol Playing Fields Society. A complimentary dinner to the touring team to be provided at the close of the match at Leeds."

One thing is certain was that Joe Platt must have wasted very little time in telegraphing the news to Houghton on the Otranto as the players were told almost on the same day as the committee made the decision. Once it became common knowledge that the two games were to be staged, Claude Avery, Bert Avery's brother, contacted the Northern Union. He made an offer to guarantee the exhibition game down in Plymouth. He did so because he had been captain of Plymouth Rugby Union club. The details of his offer were noted in a committee meeting on 23 August: "An offer was made by Mr Claude Avery to guarantee the match at Plymouth on 17th September between teams made up of tourists returning from Australia. He undertook to entertain teams from arriving to leaving for London on Sunday afternoon. To guarantee the Union £60 and if the gate is over £200 the Union to take ½. The offer was accepted subject that if boat was delayed in any way the match take place on the Monday."

It seems that even in celebrating a very successful first tour the Northern Union committee could not lay aside its business head. Wherever possible, things had to be done at a profit, but first and foremost to the union. However, the match in Plymouth did go ahead, Houghton must have telegraphed Platt to inform him that players were carrying injuries and replacements would be needed. The union arranged for players to travel to Plymouth to make up the numbers. The match went ahead on 17 September and was grandly styled as England versus Wales and the West. England lost 27–25. It was still a massive effort from the tourists to come straight off a six-week stint on the boat and onto the rugby field.

The tourists travelled from London to Leeds on Monday 19 September to be greeted by between 2,000 and 3,000 supporters who hailed their arrival back home. The supporters cheered their heroes all the way from the railway station to their hotel. The players were not allowed to stay there for long because they were needed to play a last match. The game was then played at Headingley where the tourists put out a strong side to face the Colonials.

Tourists: J. Sharrock (Wigan), J. Riley (Halifax), J. Lomas (Salford), B. Jenkins (Wigan), J. Leytham (Wigan), J. Thomas (Wigan), F. Smith (Hunslet),
F. Webster (Leeds), A. Avery (Oldham), W. Winstanley (Leigh), W. Jukes (Hunslet), F. Shugars (Warrington), H. Kershaw (Wakefield).
Colonials: H. Turtill (St Helens), A. Rosenfeld (Huddersfield), S. Deane (Oldham), J. Devereux (Hull), G. Smith (Oldham), L. Todd (Wigan),
E. Anlezark (Oldham), C. Seeling (Wigan), W. Johnston (Wigan), A. Waddell (St Helens), F. McCabe (Oldham), L O'Malley (Coventry). W. Travarthen (Huddersfield).
Referee: G.F. Dickinson (Halifax)

Around 4,000 turned up to watch the game and saw the tourists go in at half-time leading 12–5. It was a magnificent first half performance under the circumstances. But they could not sustain it and eventually lost 31–15. For the tourists, Lomas, Bert Jenkins and Leytham all scored tries which Lomas converted. The Colonials saw Smith score a couple of tries as did Lance Todd while Anlezark, Seeling and Johnston also scored, Jum Turtill kicking five goals. It was hardly surprising after six weeks at sea and little or no training that the tourists lost, but the players were happy because they got a share of the takings of £133.

Three months later, the teams met again at Wigan on 27 December. This time, a crowd of 8,000 saw the Tourists win 40–22.

After the first game there was a dinner and speeches were made. The general consensus was that that once the players had found their feet in Australia and become used to the firmer grounds and the different interpretations of the rules by the Australian referees, they had played very well indeed. Interestingly, when Houghton spoke he said that they had travelled some 34,000 miles in five months. He also made reference to the infamous match early in the tour against the Metropolis. He said that the tourists were reduced to 11 men after just 20 minutes and had still won the match.

There was something about that particular match which rankled, both with the Australian League and Northern Union. Certainly the criticism the tourists received angered both Houghton and Clifford.

When the dust settled, the players were back with their families and playing for their clubs once more, the Northern Union revealed the balance sheet for the tour. The total receipts were almost £12,000, a tremendous amount of money in 1910. Of that, the hosts retained around 40 per cent. The total expenses for the tour were stated as around £5,600 leaving the Union with an overall profit of £1,500. One third of this went to the Union, one third to the players and one third to developing the game in Australia and New Zealand. The Northern Union decided to round up the percentage of the profits going to the players so that each of them received and pocketed a magnificent £30 each, rounded up from £25/7s/5d to go with the experience of a lifetime they had enjoyed. Perhaps that was why they quite willingly played in hastily arranged matches up and down the eastern coastline of Australia? They must have been extremely pleased with the whole experience and the payment they received for their efforts. The annual wage for a labourer in 1911 was £74, and for a skilled building worker £105, so £30 was a substantial sum.

All-in-all the tour was a success on every front, the test series had been won and the test match in New Zealand won. It was, however, much more than that. The tour had cemented the Northern Union in the forefront of the sporting scene in Great Britain. It had strengthened the domestic game much to the chagrin of rugby union and established its own international credentials. The tour had shown rugby union that the Northern Union had an international stage on

125

which to perform. In fact, given the ongoing problems with amateurism that rugby union was experiencing, their international scene was little better than that of the Northern Union at that time. The Scottish and Irish unions were not prepared to play against Australia and New Zealand, considering them to be professional because they were still paying three shillings a day expenses to their players while on tour. They felt the game should be truly amateur and players receive not one penny for their efforts.

In Australia, it had driven the final nail into rugby union's claims to be the leading football code in New South Wales and established the Northern Union as the dominant winter sport in New South Wales and Queensland, a position it has never lost. It caused the rugby union in that country to become a game watched by a few diehard supporters. It took that sport a long time to recover from the blows rained on it by the tour. The players had won their battles and the war and now felt they were getting adequate recompense for their efforts on the field. They also felt they were being well looked after when injured as a result of playing the game. The public in Australia had a game to watch which was better suited to them and their ethos. They liked the action they saw on the field and that the game was in control of its own affairs. They were pleased they were not being dictated to by the RFU in London.

In New Zealand, to be fair, the tour helped to strengthen the position of the game in the Auckland area, but little else. The failure to tour the South Island, was in hindsight a major blunder which held up the progress of the game in that country. The New Zealand Rugby Union officials had seen what was happening in Australia. They had seen the New South Wales Rugby Union reduced almost to bankruptcy in a very short period of time and feared the same could happen to them. They tried to get the RFU to change the rules to make the game more appealing to spectators in the colonies. They were trying to combat the inroads the new code had made in Auckland and were terrified that its influence would spread to other areas of the country.

They also knew that once spectators saw the new code of rugby in the flesh, they would be attracted to it. It was a type of game that appealed to the New Zealand people just as it appealed to the Australians. They must have been greatly relieved when the news was released that the tourists would not visit the South Island.

Still, Albert Baskerville's decision to organise a tour to England in 1907 altered the direction of rugby league. It changed it from a

126

seemingly parochial game, in danger of dying a slow lingering death, to the vibrant world game of today, which is now growing internationally, year on year. Where would rugby league have been without Baskerville's tour? Where would New Zealand Rugby League be today, had he not been struck down so tragically young? Perhaps he would have made even more changes to our game. He talked of taking his tourists to America once the dust had settled on the All-Gold tour. Who knows what he would have achieved in that country?

We shall never know the answers to those questions. For now we can only look back after 100 years on that first ever tour to Australia and New Zealand by the Northern Union and say it was a job well done. So thanks go to the players and managers who went down under. Also our thanks go to those brave men who back in 1909 and 1910 took the momentous decision to send a team on that first ever tour, our game has become much the richer for it.

Appendix 1: The tourists

The pen pictures given here in italics are taken verbatim from the 1910 tour brochure written and published by the *Athletic News* at the behest of the Northern Union. They are the words of 'Forward' who was the rugby league correspondent for the paper. It was felt that pen pictures written 100 years ago would be more in keeping with the flavour of the book. It is interesting to note that throughout the text the 1907–08 Baskerville tour party is always referred to as the 'All Blacks', never the All-Golds. So whenever a player played in a test against those tourists we see the term All-Black. We now know that the term All-Gold was once a derogatory term rather than the term of endearment it is today to Baskerville's tourists.

The other note of interest is that at this time in Northern Union teams the backs were considered to be a more important part of the team than the forwards. For this reason, even though they were playing in the same team, the forwards would usually be paid less for each match than were the backs. When the pen pictures in the brochure were put together, generally speaking, each of the backs was allocated half of a page, while each forward was only allocated one quarter of a page. It would seem that even when putting together information about the players selected for the tour this discrimination was still maintained, although it is not known whether this was by the writer or at the behest of the Northern Union Committee.

Albert Avery
Forward
Age: 26. Height: 5 feet 10¼ inches. Weight: 14 stone 4 pounds. Club: Oldham (England international). Born: Buckfastleigh.

The record scoring forward of the Union. Has scored 13 tries in 13 successive games this season, but the number proved fatal to his record. Played for Plymouth and Devonport Albion and then migrated to Oldham. Selected for four International trial games by the Rugby Union, played for Devonshire 23 times and for Lancashire on five occasions. A useful man anywhere and has done his duty in every position possible for a rugby player.

Avery remained with Oldham until the outbreak of the First World War. After the tour his form was such that he kept his place in the first team, rarely ever missing a game, and so much so that in his last season he played 35 out of a possible 40 matches for his club. Unfortunately in the close season in 1914 he was taken ill. It turned out to be quite serious and, in an effort to help him, such was the regard for him at Oldham, the club organised a benefit match. On 14 September 1914 a team of 1910 tourists played a Colonial team at

Watersheddings. Sadly Avery died on 14 November 1914 just a year after his brother had died in similar circumstances, he was only 30. He played 289 times for Oldham, scoring 67 tries.

John Bartholomew

Threequarter
Age: 22. Height: 5 feet 8¾ inches. Weight: 11 stone 7 pounds. Club: Huddersfield (No representative honours). Born: Morecambe.

Right wing threequarter or full-back. Was the last player selected by the committee, but his abilities must not on this account be lightly valued. He came to Fartown from Morecambe and soon established himself in the affections of the Huddersfield supporters by his wonderful aggressive display. He mixed up defence with attack with such persistency that few were surprised when during the early months of the season he established a record by scoring five tries in five successive games. What is more to the point also is that three tries were in cup ties and a full-back who so departs from the orthodox is well worthy of the highest honours.

When he returned home he continued to play for Huddersfield and played in three Yorkshire Cup Finals, winning two. Sadly, he found it increasingly difficult to get a place in the 'Team of all Talents' that dominated the game prior to the First World War and in March 1914 he was transferred to Bradford Northern. He made 187 appearances for Huddersfield, scoring 41 tries and 51 goals. He continued to play for Bradford after the war and his last appearance was in 1922. He played 122 games for Bradford, including war-time friendlies, scoring 14 tries and two goals. Perhaps his greatest claim to fame in the eyes of many people was that he was the uncle of the great comedian Eric Morecambe.

Billy Batten

Threequarter
Age: 20. Height: 5 feet 10½ inches. Weight 13 stone 4 pounds. Club: Hunslet (England international). Born: Kingsley.

Left wing threequarter back and the 'hurdle jumper' of the team. Colonial full-backs beware of Batten's jump! His style is in direct contrast to that of Leytham. But none the less effective. He suffered the usual ups and downs during his junior career but went from Kingsley to Ackworth United, and ultimately arrived at Parkside. Is the most determined and dangerous (to defenders) three-quarter back in the Northern Union. County honours for Yorkshire. International for England against 'All Blacks' 'Kangaroos' and Wales. A useful man in more than one position behind the scrimmage,

and has with success played throughout a game at full-back. Holds the Hunslet club record for tries scored in one season.

Batten did not go on to tour Australia again because he refused to play in a trial match for the 1920 tour, feeling that the selectors knew his abilities. In club rugby he left Hunslet in 1913, having made 169 appearances, scoring 96 tries. He moved to Hull, for whom he made 226 appearances, contributing 89 tries. He later played for both Wakefield and Castleford, making 80 and 8 appearances respectively. Batten was not just a try scorer, but also made space for others around him to score. He played 10 tests for Great Britain, the final one in 1921, 15 matches for England and 19 times for Yorkshire.

His three sons, Eric, Bob and Billy all went on to play top-class rugby league. His great grandson Ray Batten also played at the highest level for Leeds.

Francis Boylen
Forward
Age: 28. Height: 5 feet 8½ inches. Weight: 13 stone
5 pounds. Club: Hull (England international). Born:
East Hartlepool.

Forward. Gone forward since the day he first played for Hartlepool Excelsior Juniors. Travelled to the English rugby union team via Hartlepool Old Boys and Hartlepool Rovers. County honours for Durham, seasons 1903 [to] 1908 inclusive and assisted his county to win the championship in 1905 and 1907. Played for England against France, Wales, Ireland and Scotland, and against the 'Kangaroos' for the Northern Union in the test games last season and against Wales this season. Played for Durham against Amateur 'All Blacks' and South Africa.

Boylen remained with Hull until 1912, when he was transferred to York. While at York he made 43 appearances scoring only one try. In April 1914 he was on the move once more, this time to Hull KR, where he made 38 appearances. With the outbreak of war he guested for his original club, Hull, 41 times, and on a number of occasions played for them in local derby games against his own club Hull KR. He retired after making 222 first-class appearances

Ephraim Curzon
Forward
Age: 26. Height: 5 feet 11 inches. Weight: 14 stone. Club: Salford (Lancashire County). Born: Crumpsall.

The soldier forward. Previously played for Carlisle, Lisimore and Kirkcaldy, scoring in 1907–1908 23 tries for the latter club. Served his country during the South African war and played for a representative army side against South Africa, scoring both tries in the match. County honours for Lancashire. Came to Salford last season and has never since missed a match.

With the tour completed Curzon seems to have quickly faded from the rugby league scene. As the 1910–11 season was coming to its close in April, he made his last appearance for Salford against Hull KR. They retained his playing registration until 1915, but he never played again. In total he made 102 appearances for the club scoring eight tries. He only played three seasons at Salford and was still only 27 when he played his last game. There was never any report of him being seriously injured and forced to retire. Maybe business or work interests were such that they forced him to give up the game.

James Davies
Half-back
Age: 24. Height 5 feet 8½ inches. Weight 11 stone 8 pounds. Club: Huddersfield (Wales international). Born: Swansea.

Stand-off half-back. A player who invariably pleases and behind forwards who heel out the ball provides opportunities which are a source of pleasure alike to home supporters and three-quarter backs. Was a player of repute when he came to Huddersfield and had some seasons of good service to his credit at Swansea. A special Fartown favourite. County honours for Yorkshire and played for Wales against England.

Davies remained with the very successful Huddersfield club winning every honour the game had to offer. In the 1911–12 season he became the first Welshman to score more than 200 points in a season in the Northern Union. He was an integral part of the great 'Team of all talents' that dominated the game just prior to the First World War He played his final game for the club in April 1920, notching up 265 appearances. On retiring he became the coach at Keighley.

Fred Farrar
Threequarter
Age: 25. Height: 5 feet 8½ inches. Weight: 10 stone 10 pounds. Club: Hunslet (Yorkshire County). Born: Farsley.

Right wing threequarter back. Played 10 matches with Bramley before the Hunslet officials secured his transfer to Parkside. A young man who has lost little time in preliminaries, and his first appearance in the Hunslet threequarter line was a pronounced success. County honours for Yorkshire and played for the 'Tykes' against the All Blacks and Kangaroos and was reserve for England against New Zealand. Is a particularly speedy back, can swerve to perfection, and a most consistent scorer. Earned the approval of 'Bumper' Wright who, after witnessing his first Northern Union game, Leeds [versus] Hunslet, complimented Farrar on scoring a try after a brilliant run the entire length of the field.

On his return Farrar continued to be a prolific try scorer with Hunslet. In the 1910–11 season he crossed for 17 tries and the following season bagged 24. Midway through the 1912–13 season the club decided he was surplus to requirements and he was transferred to Keighley. In total he was to make 193 appearances for Hunslet scoring 120 tries and 91 goals giving him a points total of 542 for the club. During the war he turned out once more for them as a guest even though still on Keighley's books.

Tom Helm
Forward
Age: 24. Height: 5 feet 10½ inches. Weight: 13 stone 2 pounds. Club: Oldham (Scotland [RU] international). Born: Hawick.

Forward. The only representative of Scotland on the team. Came to Oldham from the Hawick club, and before deciding upon the Northern Union game had so progressed in the rugby union as to secure his place in the South of Scotland team.

Helm remained with Oldham, but the evidence would suggest that he never fully recovered from the knee injury he sustained on tour. It was December before he was fit enough to take the field again. His last appearance for the club was in April of the following year against Runcorn. He played 43 matches for the club, scoring six tries. Helm was then allowed to sign for the newly formed Coventry NU club along with a number of other Oldham players. Sadly, the record shows that he never played for the Midlands club and he faded out of the game.

Bert Jenkins
Threequarter
Age: 25. Height: 5 feet 8 inches. Weight: 12 stone 10 pounds. Club: Wigan (Wales international). Born: Troedyrhiw.

Centre threequarter back, first played with the club of his native village, Troedyrhiw. As now, he was a success and soon came promotion to Mountain Ash. Six seasons ago he came to Wigan, and Leytham owes much to his clever centre. Has county honours for Lancashire. International for Wales, and played in the Northern Union test games against the All

Blacks and the Kangaroos. Captained the team in the match last year at Park Royal and played in all the finals for Wigan when they won their four cups last season. Is equally reliable when defensive play is necessary, and much of Wigan's success during their record season was due to his determined tackling.

Bert Jenkins toured Australia again in 1914. He remained with Wigan throughout his career and in 1921 shared a benefit match with Johnny Thomas and Dick Ramsdale, his fellow tourists. During his career for Wigan, which spanned from 1904 to 1920, he made 389 appearances scoring 182 tries. He died on 4 February 1943 aged just 59.

Chic Jenkins
Threequarter
Age: 28. Height: 5 feet 8 inches. Weight: 11 stone 6 pounds. Club: Ebbw Vale (Wales international). Born: Cwm.

Centre threequarter back and unquestionably the leading player attached to the professional rugby clubs in South Wales. Made his name when playing with Pontypool and can boast a record of 101 points scored in one season. County honours for Monmouthshire prior to signing for the Hull Northern Union club. The Boulevard at Hull, however, did not tend to develop his natural abilities. This is a nice way of saying that the Hull players failed to recognise a great player, for Chic secured his transfer and returned to his native clime, and joined newly formed Ebbw Vale club, his progress was rapid in the extreme. Gained international honours for Wales against All Blacks, Kangaroos and England.

Chic Jenkins suffered from being both a Welsh centre threequarter and having the same name as his more illustrious countryman Bert Jenkins, the Wigan centre. Having left Hull in 1907, on his return to Wales he remained with Ebbw Vale until the end of the 1911–12 season. Then sadly the Welsh club collapsed unable to compete financially with the rest of the Northern Union. With its demise Jenkins also appears to have faded out of the game.

Billy Jukes
Forward
Age: 27. Height: 5 feet 8½ inches. Weight 12 stone 10 pounds. Club: Hunslet (England international). Born: Featherstone.

Forward and the only representative of the 'terrible six'. Was a prominent scrummager with Featherstone Rovers prior to joining his present team. Has played regularly for Yorkshire since 1906–7 and opposed the Kangaroos in every representative game last season. International honours for England against Wales and the Kangaroos.

Jukes remained with Hunslet for the whole of his career and when the Australian tourists arrived in the 1911–12 season he would once again prove a thorn in their side. On 21 October 1911 he scored the try which secured a 3–3 draw for the Parksiders against the tourists. During his career with the club spanning 15 years he made 281 official appearances for Hunslet and 26 in wartime matches, a total of 307 top-flight games for them. During that time he crossed for 95 tries and kicked just three goals. Jukes was one of the game's greats of this era.

Herbert (Harry) Kershaw
Forward
Age: 25. Height: 5 feet 8 inches. Weight: 12 stone. Club: Wakefield Trinity (No representative honours). Born: Wakefield.

Forward. Joined the Wakefield Rugby Club in 1904 and the following season had the honour of playing for Yorkshire at half-back. In 1906 he signed for Wakefield Trinity and played for three seasons in the intermediate division with conspicuous success. When the Cup ties came along he was installed in the forward line, where he distinguished himself in the semi-final and final ties.

Harry Kershaw made 132 appearances for Wakefield Trinity, scoring 15 tries and seven goals. He was given a joint benefit with George Taylor by the club in 1921, and 10,000 saw the match, against Batley. John Lindley, in his history of the club, describes him as a "modest and very amiable man" and "one of the great figures" in the club's history.

James Leytham
Threequarter
Age: 30. Height: 5 feet 9 inches. Weight: 12 stone 8 pounds. Club: Wigan (England international). Born: Lancaster.

Left wing threequarter back, whose wonderful scoring has been the most effective force in bringing the Wigan club to its present position. Once Leytham thought of joining Oldham, but fortunately for Wigan the idea did not fructify. Yet it was a near thing when Leytham left Lancaster during the season of 1903–4. Records are convincing, and during the seven seasons with Wigan, Leytham has exceeded one thousand points. On December 27 last, against St Helens, he placed his 200th goal and scored his

200th try for Wigan, and is still each week piling on points. Last season was his best, and in all games for Wigan he scored 255 points. The All Blacks remember Leytham as the man who did at Central Park for 'Bumper' Wright's men lost their wonderful record that day.

Leytham did not tour again and remained at Wigan until 1911 when injury forced him to retire. In a Wigan career lasting eight years he made 280 appearances and scored a phenomenal 258 tries along with 267 goals for a career points total of 1,308. His try-scoring rate was exceptional and only bettered by a few others to have donned the cherry and white of Wigan. Sadly he was killed in a boating accident on the River Lune estuary on Sunday 20 August, 1916; he was just 36 years old.

James Lomas

Threequarter
Age: 30. Height: 5 feet 7 inches. Weight: 13 stone 3 pounds. Club: Salford (England international). Born: Maryport.

Centre threequarter back, full-back or half-back as the circumstances demand. Was a fully fledged senior before he was 16, secured county honours for Cumberland at 19, and then went to Bramley. Yorkshire county were anxious to utilise his services but the qualification rule prohibitive, and then Salford came into the question. County honours followed for Lancashire, but in latter seasons Lomas elected to play for his native county. Has secured every honour possible to a Northern Union player, and for the 15 years he has been playing football has been chief scorer each year for his club. Space prevents much reference to his wonderful records, but in 45 games for Salford Lomas has scored every point. Against Liverpool City he made 38 points and against Goole in a cup-tie 36.

Lomas returned to Salford after the tour, but not for long. In 1901 when Salford paid Bramley £100 for his services it was a record transfer fee. Lomas had made only 31 appearances for the Yorkshire club prior to his transfer. Ten years later he set the record once more, for in 1911 Oldham paid a record £300 for his services. He went on to make 80 appearances for the club, scoring 38 tries and 37 goals in the process. As the 1913–14 season was about to start he was once more transferred, this time to York. He played for them 52 times before returning as a coach at Salford. In 1922–23 he played in some cup matches for Salford, and in 1923–24 was once more forced into action, playing a couple of times. His last match was at Wakefield on 29 September 1923, at the age of 43. In total he made 312 appearances for Salford scoring 1,570 points in that time. Overall he made 426 first class appearances in a career spanning from 1901 to 1923.

Tommy Newbould

Half-back
Age: 27. Height: 5 feet 6 inches. Weight: 12 stone. Club: Wakefield Trinity (England international). Born: Castleford.

Scrummage half-back and the greatest rival to Anlezark in the Northern Union. Made himself famous in the rugby union when playing for Castleford Parish Church and Castleford. County honours for Yorkshire under both Unions, and International for England against the 'Kangaroos' and Wales. Is a man of few words and only talks on the football field. Even there his conversation is strangely limited, and opponents would welcome 'more talk and less work'. Tommy is the Wakefield pet, and in the Yorkshire Cathedral city is regarded as the player of the team. He means to do his best, and should his tries be few, others on the side will owe much to Newbould's wonderful powers.

Tommy Newbould is remembered at Wakefield Trinity for his half-back partnership with Harry Slater. Whereas Slater was of slight build, Newbould was a pocket barrel at only 5 feet 6 inches high, but weighing 12 stones. The Wakefield club history says that he "used his strength to great advantage near the line. He made 64 appearances for Trinity, scoring 26 goals and six tries. He retired at the end of the 1914–15 season.

Dick Ramsdale

Forward
Age: 24. Height: 6 feet 1 inch. Weight: 14 stone 10 pounds. Club: Wigan (Lancashire county). Born: Wigan.

Forward, the tall man of the team. Modest in all things pertaining to his football career. He went to Wigan from the Platt Bridge Junior team and growing in height, weight and ability, was soon promoted to the senior thirteen. In due course secured his cap for Lancashire. Scored 27 points for Wigan last season.

Ramsdale stayed at Wigan for the whole of his career and toured down under once more. Having signed for the cherry and whites in 1905 from junior club Platt Bridge he played until he retired in 1920. In his 15 years with the club he made 313 appearances and scored 35 tries. He died on 10 June 1933 at the age of 48.

136

Joe Riley

Threequarter

Age: 27. Height: 5 feet 9½ inches. Weight 13 stone. Club: Halifax (Yorkshire county). Born: Sowerby Bridge.

Centre threequarter back, is often confused with 'Jack' Riley the old Halifax forward, playing with Sowerby Bridge, when they joined the Northern Union in 1889. The following season found him at Halifax where he went on to fill the role of half-back, but subsequently appeared at centre, where he made such a hit that on four or five occasions he appeared in the position for Yorkshire. Captained the Halifax team in 1906–07. Since October last he has played as stand-off half-back and in his first 30 games this season he scored twelve tries and one goal. He has given of his very best in the current campaign. Equally good in attack and defence, and a most dangerous man behind the pack. A resolute tackler, a judicious provider, and one of the idols of the Halifax crowd.

On his return home, Joe Riley continued to play for Halifax. Unfortunately, while playing against Bradford in January 1915 he suffered a badly broken leg which ended his 14 year career at Thrum Hall. He played 419 times for the club scoring 117 tries along with 23 goals. In 1920 he was awarded a joint benefit with Asa Robinson, more than 20,000 turned out to honour them and he received £420. He died in March 1950 at the age of 67 and was buried in Sowerby Bridge cemetery.

George Ruddick

Forward

Age: 29. Height: 5 feet 10 inches. Weight: 13 stone 4 pounds. Club: Broughton Rangers (Wales international). Born: Brecon.

Forward. First fancied the association game, but soon transferred his affections to the Brecon rugby team. Was little known when he came to Broughton 10 years ago, but his abilities soon brought him to the front. Has been the leading forward at Broughton for many years and the most successful scoring scrummager for five seasons. County honours for Lancashire and was capped for Wales when the Northern Union discovered that George was a Welshman. Played in two test games against the All Blacks.

Like many others on the tour Ruddick remained a one club player. He saw out the remainder of his illustrious career with Broughton, picking up in the process Lancashire Cup and Challenge Cup winners' medal. His career, which had begun in 1899, ended in 1915. He played 422 times for the club. In the First World War he was wounded and badly injured a foot which meant he was unable to play again.

Jim Sharrock
Full-back
Age: 27. Height 5 feet 8 inches. Weight: 14 stone. Club: Wigan (England international). Born: New Springs Aspull.

Full-back, a player who has jumped from club football to international honours without the usual tests. Much talked of last season during Wigan's remarkable run of successes, but then Lancashire boasted two great rear men in Gifford of Barrow and Clarkson of Leigh. His club displays were absolutely convincing and his admirable defence was supplemented by aggressive play of the highest order. Sharrock was the coming man and was selected for the second International with Wales this season. Has never yet played for Lancashire and his club connection is likewise limited, for Sharrock has never yet changed his club jersey and hopes to finish his football career wearing the 'cherry and white'.

True to his word, Sharrock played his whole career for the cherry and whites making 278 appearances, scoring seven tries and 135 goals. He retired in 1912, five years later joined the Wigan board of directors and later had a spell as secretary-manager with Rochdale Hornets. He died in the 1940s.

Frank Shugars
Forward
Age: 29. Height: 5 feet 11 inches. Weight: 14 stone 6 pounds. Club: Warrington (Wales international). Born: Pontypridd.

Forward, played with the Penygraig club prior to falling a victim to the persuasive powers of the Warrington secretary. County cap for Glamorgan, and his powerful scrimmaging gained him reserve honours for Wales. Played for Lancashire and Wales under Northern Union rules.

On his return home Shugars continued to give sterling service to the Warrington club. He played on until the end of the 1911–12 season and played his last match on 27 March 1912. In a career spanning eight years he made 212 appearances and crossed for 18 tries in the process. Shugars was the club's first ever tourist and was one of the first players initiated into its Hall of Fame.

138

Fred Smith

Half-back
Age: 25. Height: 5 feet 6 inches. Weight: 12 stone 5 pounds. Club: Hunslet (England international). Born: Woodlesford.

Will either work the scrimmage or play as stand-off half-back, and is a useful man in either position. His club connection is confined to Hunslet. County honours for Yorkshire and played for England against Wales last December. Is more than usually successful at breaking through, for he scored 16 tries in the season of 1907–08.

Smith played for Hunslet for the whole of his career, which spanned around 15 years, just like his team mate Billy Jukes.

He was a prolific try scorer, but was also a great creator of tries and was known as a grafter. He toured Australia again in 1914 and became the only player in Hunslet's history to make two Lions tours. On the 1910 tour, he played in all five test matches, and won four more caps for Great Britain, as well as seven for England.

At the end of his career in 1920 the club organised a benefit match for him and Billy Jukes. Billy Batten put together a team of former Hunslet players to oppose a Hunslet side. Albert Goldthorpe agreed to turn out at the age of 48 and dropped a goal in the match for Batten's XIII. When he finally hung up his boots Smith had made 319 first class appearances for the club.

Johnny Thomas

Half-back
Age: 25. Height: 5 feet 7 inches. Weight: 11 stone. Club: Wigan (Wales international). Born: Aberkenfig.

Stand-off half-back, played rugby football before parental authority regarded him as fit to wear long trousers. While a mere stripling he played full-back for the Maesteg club. One day the officials wanted a half-back. They thought of Johnny and he worked the scrummages. Honours came fast, for he played full-back in a Welsh trial game, and in 1903 was half-back with Gwent in the trial game at Neath. Wigan officials saw him play for Glamorgan against Devonshire. They wanted Johnny, but he thought Cardiff was preferable to Central Park. However, after a famous game with Llanelli, Johnny came north and in 1904 donned the Wigan jersey. County honours for Glamorgan and Lancashire, international cap for Wales against England, All Blacks, and for the Northern Union in the test matches in 1908–09 scored 144 points and will do it again this season.

Thomas, like his Wigan tour partners, remained at the club throughout his career. He made 388 appearances and scored 1,202 points, in the process

139

crossing for 108 tries. He retired in 1919 and eventually joined the Wigan board of directors. He died on 25 September 1954, aged 73.

William Ward

Forward
Age: 21. Height: 5 feet 10 inches. Weight: 13 stone 4 pounds. Club: Leeds (No representative honours). Born: Whitehaven.

A genuine Cumberland scrummager possessed of the typical North-country grip when hard tackling is a necessity. Has lost little time in working to the front, and prior to sojourning at Headingley did useful service with Whitehaven and Egremont.

Ward played a significant part in Leeds's early history in the Northern Union. He spent 13 years with the club in an exceptional career. He made 318 appearances, scoring 99 tries and kicked one goal. His only major honour was a Challenge Cup winner's medal, in 1910.

Fred Webster

Forward
Age: 27. Height: 5 feet 9 inches. Weight: 13 stone 4 pounds. Club: Leeds (Yorkshire County). Born: Chesterfield.

Forward. A genuine front-rank man who persists to the end. Was a determined scrummager when he played with the Brotherton Juniors clubs and when the Headingley officials secured their man they quickly recognised his worth. County honours with Yorkshire and played for England against the Other Nationalities in 1905–06. Last season scored eight tries for Leeds and during the second portion of the present season's campaign has captained the side.

Webster, like many of the tourists, was a one club player. He spent 18 years at Headingley and made 543 appearances for the club. During all that time, he only won one trophy, the Challenge Cup in 1910 when he captained the side. He played in two Yorkshire Cup finals losing both to Huddersfield. He does hold one Leeds record when, in 1912–13, against Coventry, he scored eight tries in one match in a 102–0 win. This was later equalled by Eric Harris. He played for the club in the First World War, and was given a benefit match in 1919. Overall, he scored 76 tries for Leeds and kicked four goals. He was named as one of the club's Millennium Legends in 1999.

Bill Winstanley
Forward
Age: 24. Height: 5 feet 9 inches. Weight: 13 stone 9 pounds.
Club: Leigh (Lancashire County). Born: Platt Bridge.

Forward, learned the art of effective scrimmaging with the Platt Bridge junior team. Came to Leigh four years ago and now the leading forward of the side. County honours for Lancashire and secured his International cap last season.

When he returned from the tour to Leigh, following the success he had on the tour, he was quickly recruited by near neighbours Wigan. Wigan were one of the strongest outfits in the Northern Union, consequently Winstanley never had the same success with them as he had with Leigh. He found it both difficult to break into the team and to hold down a place when he did. He only made 64 appearances in seven years at Central Park.

Frank Young
Full-back
Age: 25. Height: 5 feet 7 inches. Weight: 12 stone 8 pounds.
Club: Leeds (Wales international). Born: Cardiff.

Full-back. Was a famous player before he embraced professionalism, for he came to Leeds after serving London Welsh, Bristol and Cardiff. County honours for Glamorgan and played for Wales against Scotland under rugby union rules. His club form has been capital all the season, but his display for Wales against England at Wakefield was perfection and he took the 'official eye' during that game. It is said that Young was once in the train en route for Oldham, for like Leytham, he thought the Watersheddings enclosure best suited to his abilities. However, he changed his mind, and Oldham's lost was Leeds gain.

Frank Young was badly injured in the infamous match against the Metropolis on his second outing and did not play again on the tour. On his return he continued to play at Headingley and made 159 appearances for the club, kicking 122 goals, and only scoring one try. The highlight of his career, apart from tour selection, was kicking seven goals in the Challenge Cup Final replay against Hull just prior to going on the 1910 tour. His only match for Great Britain was in 1908. He never really recovered from his injury on the tour, and retired in March 1911. He had signed for the club in January 1906 for a signing-on fee of £70.

The tour managers

Joseph H. Houghton
(St Helens)

Northern Union president. Secretary and joint manager for the tour. Holds high office for the second time, the first occasion being in 1902. Is the Lancashire County treasurer (elected 1902) and honorary secretary to the Northern Rugby League (elected 1903). A vice-president of the Lancashire and Cheshire Referees' Society and was president of the Lancashire County Union in 1900–01. Was the representative of the St. Helens club during the latter part of the first season of the Northern Union and is next in seniority to Messrs Platt, Nicholl and Smith, the three stalwarts who took office when the Union was established. One of the oldest members of the St Helens club, and was secretary for 10 years. In 1908 the members showed their appreciation by electing him to life membership, the greatest honour they could bestow for years of loyal service.

John Clifford
(Huddersfield)

Manager and most popular official. Had experience of Rugby football as a forward with the Huddersfield second XV in 1880, but his abilities were soon recognised and promotion followed in 1881. He maintained his playing connection until 1889 and was captain of the team in 1886. For 10 years he was chairman of the Football Committee and was club representative for the Senior Competition of the Yorkshire Football Union. He occupied this position at the inception of the Northern Union and at once espoused the cause of professionalism. Was Huddersfield's first representative to the Northern Union and a member of many sub-committees. Has occupied the presidential chair of the Union and was the first president of the League, and is a member of the committee today. Has attained considerable ability at cricket, tennis, and golf, and secured fame with the Huddersfield Rifle Volunteers.

Both Houghton and Clifford returned to their respective clubs and such was the esteem in which they were held following the success of that first tour that when the 1914 tour was being put together they were both asked to repeat their efforts. Both did so and sadly had the added problem of bringing the players home to a country that was at war with Germany.

Appendix 2: Statistics and records

Results

Date	Opponents	Score	Crowd	Venue
4 June	New South Wales	14–28	33,000	Agricultural Ground, Sydney
6 June	New South Wales	20–27	40,000	Agricultural Ground, Sydney
11 June	New South Wales	23–10	27,000	Agricultural Ground, Sydney
15 June	The Metropolis	34–25	3,000	Agricultural Ground, Sydney
18 June	AUSTRALIA	27–20	44,000	Agricultural Ground, Sydney
18 June	Newcastle & District	24–8	3,000	Newcastle
22 June	Newcastle & District	40–20	3,000	Newcastle
25 June	Queensland	33–9	8,000	Exhibition Ground, Brisbane
27 June	Kangaroos	10–22	28,000	Agricultural Ground, Sydney
29 June	Queensland	15–4		Exhibition Ground, Brisbane
2 July	AUSTRALIA	22–17	18,000	Exhibition Ground, Brisbane
9 July	Australasia	13–13	44,000	Agricultural Ground, Sydney
13 July	Australasia	15–32	13,000	Wentworth Park, Sydney
20 July	Maoris	29–0	2,000	Race Course, Auckland
23 July	Auckland	52–9	10,000	Victoria Park, Auckland
27 July	Rotarua	54–18	600	Rotarua
30 July	NEW ZEALAND	52–20	16,000	Domain Ground, Auckland
6 August	New South Wales	50–12	20,000	Agricultural Ground, Sydney

(NU scores first)

In Australia the tourists played 14 games, winning nine, drawing one and losing four. They scored 76 tries and 56 goals and conceded 51 tries and 47 goals

In New Zealand the tourists played four games, winning all of them. They scored 43 tries and 29 goals and conceded 11 tries and 7 goals.

Overall, they played 18 matches, won 13, drew one and lost four. They scored 119 tries and 85 goals, and conceded 62 tries and 54 goals.

Their points for and against were:

In Australia: For 340 against 247

In New Zealand: For 187 against 47

Totals for the tour: For 527 against 294

The players

Name	Club	App	Tries	Goals	Points
A. Avery	Oldham	11	7	0	21
J. Bartholomew	Huddersfield	5	3	1	11
W. Batten	Hunslet	12	5	1	17
F. Boylen	Hull	7	1	5	13
E. Curzon	Salford	6	3	0	9
J. Davies	Huddersfield	5	1	0	3
F. Farrar	Hunslet	4	4	1	14
T. Helm	Oldham	0	0	0	0
B. Jenkins	Wigan	11	14	0	42
C. Jenkins	Ebbw Vale	10	3	4	17
W. Jukes	Hunslet	12	10	0	30
H. Kershaw	Wakefield Trinity	10	5	0	15
J. Leytham	Wigan	12	12	5	46
J. Lomas	Salford	13	10	53	136
T. Newbould	Wakefield Trinity	7	2	0	6
R. Ramsdale	Wigan	7	2	0	6
J. Riley	Halifax	9	11	0	33
G. Ruddick	Broughton R	9	2	0	6
J. Sharrock	Wigan	9	0	3	6
F. Shugars	Warrington	12	1	0	3
F. Smith	Hunslet	12	4	0	12
J. Thomas	Wigan	12	7	12	45
W. Ward	Leeds	4	1	0	3
F. Webster	Leeds	14	3	0	9
W. Winstanley	Leigh	14	5	0	15
F. Young	Leeds	2	0	0	0
Guest players (versus Newcastle 18 June)					
J. Devereux	Hull	1	0	0	0
D. Frawley	Warrington	1	2	0	6
A. Morton	Hull	1	1	0	3
A.B. Burge	Souths	1	0	0	0
T. Byrne		1	0	0	0

Appendix 3: Baskerville or Baskiville?

It seems that for almost 100 years we have been spelling Albert Baskerville's name wrongly. The correct spelling is Baskiville, he on the other hand preferred to spell it Baskerville. John Haynes in his book, *From All Blacks to All Golds* suggested that the reason for this was due to the fact that he was a young upwardly mobile man and the Irish and possibly Catholic connection to Baskiville may well have prevented doors opening up to him in New Zealand. Therefore he felt the way to forge a career for himself was to anglicize the spelling.

The original family name was Baskival, it was the name of his grandfather who originated from County Mayo in Ireland. Walter Baskival served in the army for over 24 years and when he was discharged it seems he had changed the spelling of his surname to Baskivill. Walter actually moved to New Zealand as a 'Fencible', these were former soldiers who were given land outside Auckland by the government and in return helped to control the area, build and supervise roads and such like. That is how the family found themselves in New Zealand. Albert's father Henry, who was a butcher and in partnership with a man named Graves, altered the spelling once again to Baskiville. Albert for his own part, changed it yet again, to the one we all now accept of Baskerville.

Bert Baskerville was born in the small rural township of Waiorongomai and was the eldest to seven children born into the family. He left school at the age of 14 to begin working for the Auckland Post and Telegraph Office. When his father was sadly killed in an accident he became responsible of the upkeep of the family, his mother and five siblings. He was promoted in the postal service and he had to move himself and his family to Wellington,

By 1906 he had developed a reputation on the rugby field as a wing forward or wingman who was both big and quick, assets as important then as they are today. He was also a writer of note actually having a book published in 1907 on the tactics and techniques employed by the New Zealand rugby teams, it was entitled *Modern Rugby Football, New Zealand Methods*. He was a man who was destined for higher things and this as was stated earlier could well have been one of the reasons for the change to the spelling of his name.

During all of his dealings with the Northern Union and even when he published a book or signed his original All-Gold tourist contract he signed himself Baskerville. We know this was his preferred spelling by reference to the original contract signed by the players selected for the 1907 tour. A number of corrections to the spelling of players names can be seen on the original but his of Baskerville remained unaltered. These facts were unearthed by Sean Fagan and can be seen on his rl1908 website. While it seems his family agreed to his doing this in life, on his death they insisted on the correct spelling of the surname on his tombstone. Hence his tombstone reads Albert Herbert Baskiville. In respect to the great man, wherever possible in this book I have used the spelling he preferred. If it is quoted in newspaper reports used then the spelling they used was followed.

The death of Baskerville

Albert Baskerville had contracted pneumonia on the return journey to Australia after the All-Gold tour and never recovered. On their return journey the New

145

Zealanders had again stopped off in Australia to play a number of matches. On 9 May 1908, Baskerville played and scored a try in the test match the tourists played against Australia at the Agricultural Ground.

A week later, he was too ill to sit in the stand at the Exhibition Ground in Brisbane to watch the team. He had been taken ill and rushed into hospital, having caught flu on the sea trip up from Sydney to Brisbane. He had not been feeling well for a number of weeks He was diagnosed with pneumonia and sadly died just three days later on the 20 May, he was just 25 years old.

The *Evening Post* in his native Wellington reported the event in a very off hand manner on 23 May:

New Zealand Footballers
The death of Mr Baskiville
"Owing to the death of Mr. A. H. Baskiville the "All Blacks" were desirous of abandoning the balance of their matches in Australia, but the New South Wales League, having been put to considerable expense, could not see its way to sanction this. Six members of the team, including Mr Palmer accompany the body to New Zealand. They are leaving by the Monowai tomorrow."

The official notification of his death was an insertion in the same newspaper by his family on 26 May. It was simple and made no mention of his rugby exploits in any way. It is also worth noting the spelling of his name. It simply read:

"BASKIVILLE: On Wednesday 20 May, 1908 at Brisbane Australia, of pneumonia, Albert Henry eldest son of M Baskiville, Wellington, and of late H. W. Baskiville, aged 25 years."

It really was a sad and unfitting way to bring to an end the loss of the man responsible for the inception of Northern Union rugby in New Zealand. His was a man who almost single-handedly had taken on the might of the established rugby authorities in his country. Not only that but he had suffered the wrath of the government officials, he had done so unflinchingly and steadfastly. His decision to tour the 'home' country also had a knock on effect on the Australian game. This coupled with organising a successful tour of England was a measure of his talents.

We should not be surprised by his organisational ability, after all on the death of his father he had to organise his mother, himself and his siblings and ensure the family not only stayed together, but also survived. There is a great deal of evidence to support the view that when he left for England in 1907 he had in fact left behind in New Zealand his plans for the future of Northern Union rugby in his own country, even down to the setting up of a league structure. He was also heard to say while in conversation with Massa Johnston that he intended to plan a tour to America once the dust had settled on the English tour. In fact in 1907 when the newspapers were writing of the impending All-Gold tour about his intentions to play a match in California.

It was not so strange a notion to tour the USA. When the 1910 tourists were in Australia and New Zealand rugby union sought a counter attraction to combat the league game. They organised a tour to both countries by an 'American Students' team. These were students from universities in California and were not outclassed by any of the teams they played on the tour. One wonders what success Baskerville would have had on such a tour had he lived to organise it?

Albert Baskerville's grave. (Courtesy Bernie Woods)

It is a measure of his greatness that he had these plans for the future while still introducing the game into the country. None of the newspapers, not even in Wellington, made any mention of his passing or of his funeral. At his funeral on Thursday 28 May both the rugby league and rugby union authorities in Australia sent a wreath. His home union of Wellington did not. To the credit of the union and league authorities in Australia also, on the weekend following his death all flags were flown at half mast as a mark of respect. The league players all wore black arm bands. The Wellington and New Zealand Rugby Union did nothing. Being banned for life really meant being banned for life and even after death. With his passing the game lost a potentially great administrator, had he lived there is no way of knowing just what he would have achieved in the game.

While the rugby authorities and to a certain extent the press may well have taken the view that Baskerville was 'persona non grata' his colleagues from the tour did not. They had left Australia on 7 June 1908 for Wellington and on the 13 June a benefit match was quickly arranged at the Athletic Park in Wellington to raise funds for Baskerville's widowed mother. The brief account of the match must have made uncomfortable reading for the rugby union authorities. The *Bay of Plenty Times* published the following article: "A match was played by the returning professional footballers on Saturday for the benefit of the late Mr Baskiville's mother. There was a large attendance and more than £300 was taken at the gate. The players did not attempt to make a close game of it, but aimed to show the differences in the rules. The general opinion was that play was far more spectacular and some of the alterations at least must be introduced into rugby sooner or later if the game is to hold its own. The main fact that struck everyone was the abolition of much senseless scrumming by the abolition of the line out which in itself is a vast improvement Many other small features are also the removed and play was going on the whole time without stoppages."

The players and over 6,000 spectators at least paid their last respects to Baskerville in fitting style. It's a pity the country did not follow suit. We can only guess how far he would have taken the Northern Union code in his native land, given his immense organisational abilities.

The nearest to an official obituary was published in the *New Zealand Freelance* on 30 May 1908: "The football match on Wednesday was tinged with a feeling of sadness to many people, for on that day the earthly remains of Albert Henry Baskiville who had been a prominent player in Wellington for many years – were landed from the Sydney boat. When the news of his death was flashed across from Australia followers of the rugby game and players of the same received a terrible shock, for not a hint had been received that Baskiville was ill at all. As a matter of fact, he had played in a football match only a few days before his death.

The late Albert Henry Baskiville was a man of parts, but it was as the organiser on the New Zealand team of professional footballers to play a series of matches against teams belonging to the Northern Rugby Union (England) that he came prominently before the public of the Dominion. The whole of the initial arrangements of that tour were mad by him – and splendidly made too-with the result that when the final announcement of the team was made and it left these shores, everything was in apple pie order and it reflected the greatest credit on the organiser. "He being dead yet speaketh" may be truly said of Baskiville for his book on the recently completed tour is said to be in the hands of the printer, and will be directly scatter broadcast.

As a literary man the late Albert Henry Baskiville was full of possibilities and showed much ability. His book on *Rugby Football* was widely read, his conclusions and concepts of the game as there in expressed showed the master mind. Many of his literary contributions were published in newspapers in the Dominion and the Old Country, and as a writer his career promised to be a bright one. On the football field Baskiville was a rattling good player – fast and dashy – and at the business end of a forward rush he could fall on the ball with the best of them. In the Oriental club he made many friends by the valuable assistance he rendered its senior team as a wing forward and amongst his opponents in those days he was highly esteemed for the good-tempered way in which he played the game. By profession he was a telegraph operator, and was clever in the manipulation of the Morse instrument.

At the time of his untimely death he was under leave of absence from the Head Officer of the Telegraph Department of the Dominion.

'May the earth lie lightly on the remains of the good fellow'."

The article made reference to Baskerville actually sending to the printers a book covering the tour in 1907–08. It could have been a wonderful recollection of the game then and perhaps an insight into the problems he encountered with the authorities in his home country. We do know that he did take copious amounts of notes throughout the tour, but sadly they never saw the light of day. When he died suddenly, the book died with him. Who knows, perhaps his notes are collecting dust in some Wellington attic. If they were ever to turn up they could give us great insights into the tour.

His death was a massive loss both in this country and his native New Zealand. Albert Henry Baskiville was laid to rest at Karori Cemetery on 28 May 1908 after a service at St Peters Church on Willis Street in Wellington.

Hunslet through and through

Geoff Gunney MBE, rugby league footballer

Maurice Bamford

Authorised biography of Hunslet and Great Britain star by former Great Britain
coach Maurice Bamford. Published in April 2010 at £13.95. order for just
£13.00 post free direct from London League Publications Ltd. Order from LLP,
PO Box 10441, London E14 8WR. Cheques payable to London League
Publications Ltd, credit card orders via www.llpshop.co.uk
Also available from any bookshop at £13.95 (ISBN: 9781903659465)

PETER FOX
The Players' Coach

Graham Williams & Peter Lush

Authorised biography of former Great Britain coach Peter Fox. Published in June 2008 at £14.95, special offer £10.00 post free from London League Publications Ltd. Order from LLP, PO Box 10441, London E14 8WR. Cheques payable to London League Publications Ltd, credit card orders via www.llpshop.co.uk

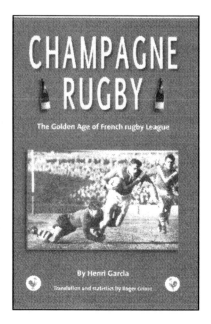